AMERICAN INTERIORS

Books by Harold L. Peterson

AMERICAN KNIVES
A HISTORY OF FIREARMS
FORTS IN AMERICA
A HISTORY OF KNIVES
A HISTORY OF BODY ARMOR
AMERICAN INTERIORS
HOW TO TELL IF IT'S A FAKE

HAROLD L. PETERSON

AMERICAN INTERIORS

From Colonial Times to the Late Victorians

A pictorial source book of American domestic interiors

with an appendix on inns and taverns

CHARLES SCRIBNER'S SONS   NEW YORK

This book published simultaneously in the
United States of America and in Canada—
Copyright under the Berne Convention

All rights reserved. No part of this book
may be reproduced in any form without the
permission of Charles Scribner's Sons

1 3 5 7 9 11 13 15 17 19   M/P   20 18 16 14 12 10 8 6 4 2

Printed in the United States of America
Library of Congress Catalog Card Number 78–71679
ISBN 0–684–16182–6 (paper)

Ad
Colonel Charles West
Optimus amicus et studiossimus rerum Americanorum

PREFACE

Looking at pictures is a diverse and personal experience. Some find in them an emotional impact, some an esthetic delight, and still others study them primarily for the information they may contain. And this, of course, varies also with the nature of the picture involved. Some score heavily on all three fronts while others touch only one or perhaps fail in all aspects with at least some of their viewers. Thus a book dealing primarily with pictures must of necessity be a very personal thing. This is certainly the case with the present volume. As a frustrated artist I am certainly not insensitive to the emotional and esthetic qualities of a picture, but the ones that I have included here have been picked entirely for the type and quality of the information that they contain.

For more than a quarter of a century as a trained historian and professional museum curator, I have concentrated on pictures as primary source material for various aspects of my work. To me it has been both a very pleasant and a highly informative research project. Since these pictures are scattered in public and private collections all over the country, it finally occurred to me that a compilation of the most meaningful ones might be of interest to others who are concerned with American social history, with the general field classified as "Americana," with interior decoration or the decorative or even fine arts. At least it would bring these pictures together in one convenient place and indicate the present location of the originals for those who might wish to study them in greater detail.

The beginning and terminal dates for this compilation may at first glance seem capricious, but there are reasons. The year 1659 results from the fact that the John Eliot portrait is the earliest painting I have been able to find that illustrates any phase or aspect of decorative practices in the American home. The terminal year of 1876 developed because it offered a logical stopping point at a period when pictures of interiors start to become so plentiful that there is a problem in selection. The centennial of America's independence in 1876 had a great impact on taste and practices. A renewed interest in forms and styles related to American history developed. Reproductions of Chippendale and "Pilgrim" styles in furniture began to take their places alongside the designs based on Jacobean, Renaissance or Louis XVI prototypes that had been popular earlier. Also there came a considerable interest in the Orient. Eastern rugs had long been popular, but now there were Japanese corners, Moorish corners, a widespread use of Japanese ceramics, Oriental screens, and a heavy emphasis on bamboo and lacquer. These and other changes began while the Centennial celebration was in progress, but did not sweep the nation overnight. Thus I have included a few interesting pictures actually painted in 1877 and even one done in 1878 because they still reflect the styles and attitudes that predominated before the great celebration.

In making my picture selections I have had to establish certain criteria. Among them, quite naturally, is the definition of the word home. For this book I have interpreted it widely as including any permanent or quasi permanent residence whether it be in a house, a barracks or even a cabin or hut. Quite arbitrarily, I have omitted the homes of Indians. Some of the very earliest pictures of American domestic interiors illustrate Indian dwellings, but they fall into an entirely different tradition and so it seemed best to confine this volume to the homes of Europeans and their descendants. Finally, I have felt that it was of the utmost importance that a picture had to be of the period it illustrated. No historical recreation, no photographs made years later of rooms that had remained "just as they were when. . . ." This is necessary, it seems to me, if the book is actually to present what historians would classify as primary source material. In addition, a picture, in order to qualify, needed to do something more than merely illustrate a piece of furniture. These have been well documented in numerous specialized books. If it indicated the use of a piece of furniture or the appearance of such ephemeral things as slipcovers, cushions or antimacassars that have not survived in such quantity, then it has been included. If it illustrated room arrangement, decorative practices, or taste in general, it was welcomed.

The pictures are arranged generally in chronological order, but there are exceptions in order to keep illustrations of related interest close together.

The 206 illustrations that I have included here are by no means all the interesting and informative pictures that exist. Some have been rejected because the information they present is largely repetitive. A few very good ones had to be omitted because either publication permission or good reproducible photographs could not be obtained. In a few instances there was a problem in dating, and I wanted to be as certain as possible that the pictures were actually completed within the period. By and large, however, these are the drawings, prints, paintings and photographs that I have found the most interesting, useful and pleasant over the years. In the captions I have tried to indicate the features of the pictures that I have found meaningful and, where pertinent, to relate them to written sources in the hope that the reader, too, will find them as enjoyable and stimulating as I have.

In a compilation of this sort, the author incurs a greater debt for the help of others than in almost any other kind of book. The collectors, museum curators, registrars and directors in charge of the pictures published here have been exceptionally gracious and kind in providing photographs, data and permission to reproduce their holdings. Although it is not adequate, the credit lines with each illustration at least indicate the individual or institution which owns the picture and to whom my sincere thanks are extended. These credit lines vary in wording at the expressed wish of each, but my appreciation is the same for all.

Many individuals have gone well beyond the call of duty in providing help, and although I cannot mention all of them individually, there are some who must be acknowledged. Among these is Kermit M. Edmonds, then of the Wyoming State Historical Museum, who volunteered to canvass museums in the West that I had not been able to visit personally in a search for possible pictures. It was a completely altruistic gesture deriving from his intense interest in museum research, and he performed it heroically to my great benefit.

Dr. Hermann W. Williams, Jr., Director Emeritus of the Corcoran Gallery of Art, not only encouraged this project from the beginning, but also made available his extensive collection of notes and photographs of American genre paintings as well as offering wise advice and shrewd suggestions for additional research.

Among the private collectors, I am especially indebted to Bertram K. and Nina Fletcher Little who made their important personal collection available to me. Col. Edgar William and Bernice Chrysler Garbisch did likewise and so did Mr. and Mrs. Samuel Schwartz, Marius B. Peladeau and my colleague, Miss Vera Craig.

Some of the private commercial galleries also extended not only courteous but enthusiastic help without any expectation of personal advantage. Among them I should especially like to thank Mr. Rudolph Wunderlich of Kennedy Galleries, Inc., New York City, Mr. Clyde Newhouse of Newhouse Galleries and Miss Mary K. Rutherford of Hirschl & Adler Galleries, both also of New York City, Miss Joan Wortsman of Maxwell Galleries, Ltd. of San Francisco and Mr. Warren Howell of John Howell Books, San Francisco.

From fellow workers in the museum field one almost naturally expects help, but again some have gone far beyond the usual courtesies. These include Mrs. Lois McCauley, P. William Filby and Miss Celia Holland of the Maryland Historical Society; Richard J. Koke and Martin Leifer of the New-York Historical Society; Frederick L. Rath, Jr. and Minor Wine Thomas of the New York State Historical Association; Albert K. Baragwanath of the Museum of the City of New York; Dr. Thomas J. McCormick of the Vassar College Art Gallery; Ian M. G. Quimby, Charles F. Hummel and Charles F. Montgomery of the Henry Francis du Pont Winterthur Museum; Clement M. Silvestro and Mrs. Paul M. Rhymer of the Chicago Historical Society; Peter A. G. Brown of the Abby Aldrich Rockefeller Folk Art Collection; Robert B. Mayo, Mrs. Robert V. Anderson and Mrs. Stuart Gibson of the Valentine Museum; Miss Rodris Roth and Peter Copeland of the Smithsonian Institution; Frederick B. Robinson of the Museum of Fine Arts of Springfield, Massachusetts; Holman J. Swinney and William K. Verner of the Adirondack Museum; Samuel Townsend of North Carolina State Department of Archives and History; George O. Bird of the Henry Ford Museum and Greenfield Village; Richard H. Randall, Jr. and William Johnston of the Walters Art Gallery; Richard E. Kuehne of the West Point Museum; and John Millie of Independence National Historical Park.

And, as always, my wife Dorothy. Although typing is no longer as easy as it once was, she still completed this entire manuscript and offered sage suggestions and criticism.

Harold L. Peterson

Arlington, Virginia

X

The American home lies at the very center of American history. Even in the years when men worked twelve to fourteen hours a day, six days a week, when frontiersmen lived months in the forests and soldiers served for years in the field, the great bulk of all Americans spent more time in their homes than anywhere else. It has always been—and still is—the center of their existence, the milieu in which they have developed their ideas and attitudes, sought their strength and comfort and built the relationships that dominated their lives. Until the present century it was a rare American who was not born at home and only a slightly less rare individual who did not die there. The church, the field and the place of business or entertainment demanded attention and service. For some they even became paramount, but for the great majority there was indeed "no place like home."

For all these years the home has been a complex thing. It has combined physical surroundings, location, emotion and inter-personal relationships among other factors that could be identified and listed *ad infinitum*. Yet the building and its contents are by no means unimportant. In their way they both reflect and condition attitudes, impose limitations and provide the environment for achievement. The person who dwells there can burgeon within it; he can triumph over it; or he can yield to its restrictions, but he cannot ignore it. He never could. This situation was the same 300 years ago as it is now. It may seem a truism, but if these premises are accepted it follows automatically that one cannot hope to understand American social history without at least a basic knowledge of the physical surroundings that comprised the American home and a sense of their significance.

Fortunately, the historian who seeks data on this important subject has a wide variety of sources to peruse. Almost as soon as the English settlers founded their first permanent settlements at Jamestown, Plymouth and Massachusetts Bay, they began to make inventories of their possessions. They did so for inheritance purposes, for taxation and eventually for insurance. These lists are highly valuable for assessing the quantity and types of furnishings that comprised an early American home, but they offer little or no information about their use or the esteem in which they were held. This void has been filled by travellers and journalists, some native and some foreign, some objective and some highly prejudiced, who reported on the homes and domestic practices that they observed. In later years elderly men and women recorded their reminiscences of the homes of their youth so that these conditioning factors should not be forgotten in a changing world. Advertisements in newspapers and catalogs provide still more information as do letters to merchants and craftsmen setting forth the writer's needs and desires. In recent years archeological explorations, too, have contributed to knowledge about American homes and their contents.

Finally there are the contemporary pictures that illustrate details of these early homes—to date the least used of all sources. It is with these pictures that the present volume is primarily concerned. Some are portraits that include information about the home by happenstance. Some are scenes deliberately recorded to offer data about a room's appearance. And still others are illustrations of events or genre scenes that reveal details of decoration, use or practice while telling a story. Each kind is useful. As long as the artist was presenting an interior of the era and area in which both he and his potential viewers lived, one can normally accept his depictions as accurate. If he portrayed a detail that everyone would know was wrong or impossible, he would be destroying the effectiveness of his picture. Under normal circumstances he would be careful not to do it. As soon as he departed from his own time and his own part of the world, however, his credibility diminishes rapidly. Odd or unusual details might deliberately be included in the striving for a quaint effect or a feeling of difference. Or errors might be introduced inadvertently through lack of knowledge.

Minor mistakes can also enter pictures for a variety of reasons. Details may be omitted because of carelessness or memory failure or they may be eliminated deliberately to avoid distracting the viewer's attention. Similarly, extra drapes or objects may be added to create a better composition. Normally, however, these

A. When an artist attempts to portray a scene in a different land and at an earlier date, his picture cannot be considered as evidence for American practices of the era. In this example Eunice Pinney's *The Cotter's Saturday Night* of about 1815 attempts to illustrate Robert Burns' earlier Scottish poem. As far as is known, no American home (and probably no Scottish home) ever looked like this.
Collection of Edgar William and Bernice Chrysler Garbisch.

additions and subtractions can be readily recognized. A little common sense plus a moderate background in period practices is all the student needs.

More important because it is more insidious is the prejudice of the artist. Often a picture is created as an editorial or a crusading document, and facts are accordingly distorted. Two cases in point are the majority of pictures that portray Negro homes and slum dwellings in big cities. Southern and pro-slavery artists tended to show the condition of the Negro in the best possible light in the days before the end of the Civil War. After that conflict they sometimes depicted him as living in squalor as if it were either of his own choosing or a hardship he now suffered because he was no longer looked after by a considerate master. Other pictures are sometimes patronizing or caricaturish. A good objective picture of a Negro home is exceptionally hard to find, but there are a few. Likewise, poverty in the 19th century was often regarded as the result of laziness and sloth. The two illustrations of slum dwellings in New York City in 1860 shown in plates 102 and 103, for instance, make it clear that the residents are Irish Catholics, a recent immigrant group with a minority religion in predominantly Protestant America. The implication that they are responsible for their own plight is very strong.

Perhaps the biggest drawback to the use of pictures as a source for a history of American homes, however, is the lack of balance. Contemporary depictions of any aspect of American domestic interiors are exceptionally rare in the 17th century. They are very scarce in the 18th century, but after 1800 they multiply in almost geometrical progression as each decade passes. The geographical balance is even worse. New England and the Middle Atlantic States are heavily represented, but pictures grow infinitely scarcer as one moves south and west. The Southwest is almost totally unrepresented before 1870, and the Far West is only slightly better covered. Similarly, there are many more pictures of upper middle class homes than those of either wealthier or poorer families. And finally, some rooms are pictured much more often than others. Living rooms, drawing rooms, or parlors come first. Libraries appear upon occasion, and with the growing popularity of the genre painting in the second quarter of the 19th century, kitchens become plentiful. Bedrooms and dining rooms are scarce throughout, and hallways and storage areas are the rarest of all.

Despite the imbalance in coverage and the possibility of accidental or deliberate error on the part of the artist, these pictures offer a source for information about the American home that is unparalleled elsewhere. No written document can offer so much data about the treatment of rooms and their contents, the details of interior decoration and taste, the use of rooms, and the exact type and quality of the furnishings found in each situation. This much is obvious to even the casual viewer. The growing quantity and diversity of fabrics, furniture, manufactured goods and decorative objects help trace the course and effects of the In-

B. Some genre painters based their works on meticulous sketches of actual scenes. Here William Sidney Mount even notes the hours during which the sunlight enters the doorway of a rough cabin.
Collection of Hermann W. Williams, Jr.

C. Even photographs can offer differing evidence. This picture was obviously taken by the same photographer and at the same time as the one in plate 122. Even the dressing gown is in the same position on the bed. But note that someone has removed the liquor bottles and other drinking paraphernalia from the table at the foot of the bed, perhaps to improve Dr. Henry's image for posterity!
Courtesy Smithsonian Institution.

XVI

dustrial Revolution and improved transportation. The ubiquitous cuspidor or spitting box in all places of public gathering and even in some bedrooms bears witness to changing social practices just as the absence of wastepaper baskets underlines a difference in living habits. In a day when most homes include at least one of these trash containers in almost every room, it comes as something of a shock to realize that the average American household did not even boast a single one until the present century. The very first wastepaper baskets appear in homes about the middle of the 19th century—and then they are confined to the studies of writers and politicians. For the average citizen open fires took care of what little scrap paper he might have. Good paper was carefully saved for reuse or sale to the rag man.

Drawing a slightly longer bow the student can also obtain inferences about such things as attitudes towards pets, flowers and growing plants and other similar subjects. There are some hazards in these fields. Depending upon the artist's skill in draftsmanship and the accuracy of his observation, however, one can usually come reasonably close in identifying at least general breeds of pets and types of flowers and so assess their relative popularity, their place in the home, and sometimes other factors as well. In the flower field, for instance, the pictures suggest that the rose maintained the highest esteem throughout the entire period. Of all the identifiable flowers, it is by far the commonest and the most prominent. Otherwise, in the 1840's and '50's, the dahlia apparently ranked higher than it does now, and former generations accorded a place in their bouquets to flowers that are now almost beyond the pale—morning glories and honeysuckle, for instance. Flower arrangements also change from the large bouquets of the early years to the small nosegays that became popular during the Victorian period. Growing plants seldom appear inside before about 1830, but thereafter they become more and more plentiful until they convert some rooms into veritable greenhouses in the 1870's.

A love of pets also seems to have been common throughout—and these pets had house privileges in all periods. Caged birds can be found at least from the early 18th century with parrots, local song birds and canaries predominating. Cats and dogs, too, seem to have been everywhere. Most of the dogs pictured look like mongrels of broad ancestry, but some clearly identifiable breeds appear also. Spaniels can be found as early as 1767, and they remain popular throughout. Soon afterwards one encounters pointers, English setters and retrievers, but before 1820 there is also a probable poodle, and in 1874 there is a very definite pug, a good decade earlier than the standard breed books state that pugs came to America. Samuel F. B. Morse offers the first pictorial evidence of a goldfish and goldfish bowl in a painting of 1835 that is now in a private collection and not available for inclusion here. Eastman Johnson portrayed an identical bowl in *Girl and Pets* in 1856 (now in the Corcoran Gallery of Art), and he also included a cat, a parrot and what looks like a pair of guinea pigs. Back in the 18th century John Singleton Copley had even showed a squirrel on a string in an interior setting. This is the limit of indoor pets according to the pictures thus far discovered, but it is an impressive list, and the prominence they are given suggests that their owners considered them very important parts of their households.

Other impressions also come sharply to mind. The eclecticism in room furnishings that appears in painting after painting is one. The furniture shown is often of widely varying ages and qualities, seldom of a single period, style or cost. A bedroom of the 1870's may have an early 18th century bed and a Chippendale wing chair along with newer pieces. A crude cabin may boast a fine piano while everything else is simple and locally made. Robert E. Lee's study at Washington College contained an old sideboard and a dining room table, pieces that no modern curator would think of putting in a refurnished study. The working kitchen that emerges from these contemporary pictures is also far different from the one encountered in most period restorations. It is an efficient area with only the needed equipment visible. There is none of the forest of kettles, toasters, reflector ovens, etc., that clutter most refurnished hearths where they would almost certainly trip any cook who tried to work there.

Equally interesting is the death blow to the standard tradition of a gun hung over the fireplace. Guns appear in many contemporary pictures, but they are normally hung over or near the door where they would be handy when a man went out. They were definitely not hung in a location where heat would dry and shrink the wood and smoke and grease would coat them. There is no early American picture thus far found that shows a gun in the traditional position on the mantel or chimney breast. One Currier & Ives print shows rifles and hunting swords hung above the mantel, but it is a copy of a scene in a European hunting lodge and so has no validity. The first picture that does show firearms clustered around the mantel is a photograph of 1872 taken in a ranch house in Idaho (plate 154). By then perhaps the tradition had become so established that reality had come to follow it.

These are just a few of the thoughts and impressions that come to mind when looking at these pictorial sources for American social history. Each viewer will discover others that have personal significance because of his background or interests—or his mood at the time. Like other types of primary source material they may profitably be plumbed time and again. But few other sources offer their raw data so attractively that one can obtain esthetic pleasure while noting the way paper covers are tied on storage jars. Here is serendipity indeed. The data are there for the student; the pleasure is there for all.

AMERICAN INTERIORS

Plate 1. *John Eliot,* artist unknown, oil, 1659. Henry E. Huntington Library and Art Gallery.

American paintings of the 17th century that illustrate any aspect of interior decoration are extremely rare, and the quality of this portrait suggests that it may well have been painted back in England on a visit by this great missionary, linguist and writer. It is a typical stylized portrait of the period with an imaginary drape and tassel in the background as well as a hypothetical bookshelf. Still, it offers pictorial evidence of contemporary practices if one looks closely.

Most important is the Oriental carpet covering the table on which he displays one of his books. "Turkey" or "Turkey work" carpets, as they were called regardless of actual origin, appear in the very earliest American household inventories. They were almost always small in size and highly prized by their proud owners who seem frequently to have included them in their portraits. They were, in fact, far too precious to put on the floor. Instead, they served as covers for tables, chests, cupboards and beds—and even as hangings on walls and at windows. And this remained true well into the next century. Other carpets in addition to Orientals were also used on tables at this period as shown by the 1653 inventory of Capt. Stephen Gill of Virginia which included "1 Small side Table & striped Carpett."

Plate 2. *Alice Mason,* artist unknown, oil, 1668. Adams National Historic Site.

Young Alice Mason, showing no evidence of the tragic life to come, here stands upon a checkered floor of a type highly popular in colonial America. Inspired by the marble and tile floors of the better European homes, these designs might be painted directly upon the wooden floorboards or on a canvas floor cloth that covered the boards in carpet fashion. The popularity of this design can be gauged by the frequency with which it appears in the American portraits of the 17th and early 18th centuries and less often even into the 19th century. In the early 1700's such floor cloths begin to appear in wills and inventories and even in newspaper advertisements. When William Burnet died in 1729, for instance, he had "two old checquered canvases to lay under a table" as well as another room-sized floor cloth of unknown design. Almost always these checkerboard floors are shown as black and white in paintings, but documents mention blue and white, yellow and black, and there is an original brown and yellow specimen in the Henry Francis du Pont Winterthur Museum.

At best, however, painted floors or floor cloths graced only the homes of the affluent minority—and then only in their best rooms. The great majority of all house floors in America were bare wood with perhaps a decorative covering of clean sand. As late as 1800 Lyman Beecher noted that his wife introduced the first painted floor cloth (which she made herself) to East Hampton, Long Island, where all the other houses "had sanded floors, some of them worn through."

Plate 3. *Isaac Royall and Family* by Robert Feke, oil, 1741. Harvard University. Law School Collection.

Isaac Royall, shown here at the age of 22 with his wife, sister, sister-in-law and daughter, was a Massachusetts magnate, a loyalist who fled to England in 1775 but who still left a bequest to Harvard that founded its Law School. Obviously a man of wealth, he here displays a fine Turkey carpet covering a table. Such carpets were still symbols of elegance as they had been when John Eliot had his portrait painted back in 1659. In England some affluent families were beginning to use these expensive fabrics as floor coverings, and the trend may have started in America as well, but it was another decade before it became at all common. Indeed, Nathan Bailey's *Universal Etymological Dictionary* of the time defined a carpet as "a Covering for the Table." It was only later that he expanded it to "a Covering for a Table, Passage, or Floor." If an American family of the mid 18th century had a floor covering it was most likely to be a painted floor cloth or an ingrain, English or "Scotch" pileless double-cloth woven carpet. The homes of average Americans and even many of the rooms of the wealthy, however, remained uncovered.

Plate 4. *Peter Manigault and His Friends* by George Roupell, black ink and wash, c. 1760. Courtesy, the Henry Francis du Pont Winterthur Museum.

If George Roupell's memory was correct, this convivial gathering in Charleston, South Carolina, was held in an exceedingly plain room with no floor covering, no hangings at the window, not even a tablecloth. Actually this situation was more common than not in mid 18th century America. There are, however, several interesting details. The coaster or bottle-stand under one of the bottles was customary; the similar feature under the punch bowl was not, as far as we know. The use of wine glasses for both punch and wine or raw drams confirms a suspected practice, and the parrot in its cage on the window ledge depicts a popular household bird of the era in a very modern-looking enclosure. George Roupell, incidentally, depicts himself with his back to the viewer at the left front corner of the table and his host Peter Manigault sits at his left with his hand around the neck of a bottle.

Plate 5. *Israel Israel* by unknown artist, oil, c. 1775. Abby Aldrich Rockefeller Folk Art Collection.

Many documents indicate the use of slip covers in Colonial America, but very few pictures show what these practical devices looked like. Here, however, Israel Israel sits proudly on a side chair of the so-called Chippendale style with a rose-colored slip cover that boasts a ruffled skirt with a fringe and what appears to be a braided or embroidered border. A close look at the portrait also reveals that the chair is placed upon a black and white checkered floor cloth exactly like that shown in plate 2 a century and more earlier.

Plate 6. *The First, Second, and Last Scene of Mortality,* a needlework picture by Prudence Punderson, late 18th century. The Connecticut Historical Society.

Prudence Punderson's unique depiction of the three major stages of life: birth and babyhood at right, adulthood in the center and death at left, also illustrates several important aspects of decoration and contemporary mores. The checkered floor in three colors suggests a more complicated floor cloth than the usual black and white. The windows boast drapes with a valance, the side pieces looped up and over tie-backs. The white embroidery over the windowpanes may perhaps suggest glass curtains which would be unusual; more likely it is an attempt to illustrate the glass itself. At the left the coffin lies on a drop-leaf table, the deceased's initials picked out in brass-headed tacks on the top. Behind it, the mirror is draped in mourning as was often done when a corpse lay in the house.

...nd Last Scene of Mortality. *Prudence Punderson.*

Plate 7. *The Samels Family* by John Eckstein, oil, c. 1788. Courtesy, Museum of Fine Arts, Boston.

John Eckstein painted in both England and America, and there is thus some doubt whether he did this picture just before or just after he crossed the Atlantic. In either case, he illustrates a fine Axminster carpet on the floor and a proper tea service arranged on the tilt-top tea table that has been pulled in front of the couch for comfortable use. The fireplace with its brass fender sports a marbleized coat of paint in keeping with the taste of the period, and there is a very interesting painted border just above the chair rail. On the wall the oval portraits and the Adam style looking glass are hung much higher than a modern decorator would feel proper, a practice that seems to have remained standard until after 1900.

Plate 8. *Congress Voting Independence* by Edward Savage, unfinished engraving after his painting, 1780–1814. Independence National Historical Park.*

The Pennsylvania Assembly Room in Independence Hall was by no means a domestic interior. It is included here only because it illustrates the use of Venetian blinds. Savage worked on his painting of this historic event for more than two decades. The engraving after it was still incomplete at his death, but it offers the clearest vision of the Venetian blinds in the windows at the left. Interestingly, these blinds appear in no contemporary picture of an American home yet discovered although documents indicate that they were known and were presumably quite popular. John Webster, an upholsterer in Philadelphia, advertised them for sale in the August 20, 1767 issue of the *Pennsylvania Journal,* and his description shows that the virtues of these versatile blinds were well understood:

> . . . , the newest invented Venetian sun blinds for windows, on the best principles, stain'd to any colour, moves to any position, so as to give different lights, screens from the scorching rays of the sun, draws cool air in hot weather, draws up as a curtain, and prevents from being overlooked, and is the greatest preserver of furniture of any thing of the kind ever invented.

Thomas Jefferson made a drawing of a Venetian blind which is now in the Massachusetts Historical Society, and this is the only other American picture of them known for this period. A final irony of this situation is that despite Savage's evidence, most modern students believe that Independence Hall actually did not have Venetian blinds in its windows in 1776!

* Although this painting is traditionally listed as a collaboration between Robert Edge Pine and Savage, recent scholarship has proved that Pine had nothing to do with it.

Plate 9. *Portrait of Chief Justice and Mrs. Oliver Ellsworth* by Ralph Earl, oil, 1792. Courtesy Wadsworth Atheneum, Hartford.

In this engaging portrait Ralph Earl has shown the Ellsworths seated in the library of their handsome white frame home (shown by artistic license through the window). Of especial interest is the upholstery of the Chippendale side chair of Judge Ellsworth with the decorative pattern of brass-headed tacks and the fringe below the seat rail, the built-in bookcase painted to match the wood trim of the room, and the carpet with its bold black, red, orange and white pattern. The window apparently had no drapes, at least in this summer scene. The bold satin or damask draperies shown at both sides of the picture existed only in the artist's mind.

Plate 10. *John Phillips* by Joseph Steward, oil, c. 1793. Courtesy the Trustees of Dartmouth College.

John Phillips of Exeter, New Hampshire, sits in a Windsor arm chair that must have been tightly squeezed between his covered drop-leaf table and his handsomely panelled walls. From a decorative standpoint, the most important aspects of the painting are the painted wall-to-wall floor cloths with their floral motifs in shades of russet, olive-green and yellow that must have been practical as well as attractive. Through the open door one can note that the adjacent room has a floor cloth of a different pattern and that the wall boasts a stenciled border around the window, at the ceiling joint, and along the top of the baseboard that almost repeats the floor covering. The fringed valance and cascades with the big tassels in solid colors offer a fine foil to the patterns of the floor and borders and help produce an exceptionally handsome room.

Plate 11. *Angus Nickelson Family* by Ralph Earl, oil, c. 1796. Museum of Fine Arts, Springfield, Massachusetts.

Angus Nickelson was a prosperous owner of an iron mill in New Milford, Connecticut, when the elder Ralph Earl painted this interesting portrait of him and his family. The wall-to-wall carpeting is typical of the best room of a fine home of the period as are the drapes with short cascades and long tassels on the numerous windows. It is interesting in this as well as numerous later paintings to note how often the windows are shown with the shutters closed. The oval looking glasses between the windows are hung on wires over ornamental hangers placed just below what appears to be a stenciled border at the top of the wall that is joined by a vertical stencil at the corner. Most interesting of all, however, is the desk with a fringed cover on its fallboard that seems to be built into a wall-size bookcase. The cylindrical pillow against the arm of the sofa is an early appearance of a feature that became especially popular early in the next century.

Plate 12.   *Samuel Griffin* by William Dunlap, oil, 1800–1809. National Gallery of Art, Washington, D. C.; Gift of Edgar William and Bernice Chrysler Garbisch.

Samuel Griffin sits in what would almost seem an austere room were it not for the colors that give it life. The carpet, cut out for the hearth and edged with an applied floral border, has a creamy yellow ground with pink and green blossoms that harmonize beautifully with the bright apple-green walls. Edging these walls are a series of stenciled or wallpaper borders with a floral design in blue, pink, red and white on a gray background. This border is double at the base of the wall where there appears to be no baseboard, single above the chair rail and around the fireplace opening and also at the top of the wall where a tiny portion of it can be glimpsed in the architecturally puzzling niche in the corner at the right. This niche seems to serve absolutely no useful purpose, but perhaps it was more decorative in real life than it appears in the painting.

In 1797 George Washington had written twice to Tobias Lear in Philadelphia asking him to obtain blue carpeting for the parlor at Mount Vernon to accord with the blue upholstery of the furniture. In this instance, Samuel Griffin's carpet complemented the wall colors, not the furniture, which is upholstered in black.

Plate 13.   *James Prince and Son, William* by John Brewster, Jr., oil, 1801. Courtesy Historical Society of Old Newbury, Newburyport, Massachusetts.

When John Brewster, Jr., painted this portrait of James Prince and his son in a small corner of the wealthy merchant's handsome brick house, he recorded two details of unusual interest. For one thing the elder Prince sits at a portable desk that rests on a small table instead of one of the slant-top desks or secretaries that might be expected in such a well-furnished home. And the table itself is also unusual. The top has been covered, probably with baize. This cover is secured with brass-headed tacks, and there is a ruffled skirt that completely hides the frame and apron of the table. Behind this portable desk is one of the more usual secretaries of the period with one door standing open to reveal the rows of books within. At the far right there is just a glimpse of the window draperies that consist of a fringed valance with cascades over panels that are also fringed and which hang like cascades without tie-backs. The floor has a carpet in shades of gray. It is probably a Wilton since the records indicate that the Princes owned two Wilton carpets of 72 yards each at this time. The date, incidentally, can be determined by the letter lying on the portable desk which is headed "Newburyport Novr. 24 1801."

Plate 14. *The Sargent Family* by an unknown artist, oil, 1800. National Gallery of Art; Gift of Edgar William and Bernice Chrysler Garbisch.

The Sargents of Massachusetts were apparently an upper middle class family who could afford many of the better things of life. The brown, tan and cream carpeting that covers the main room wall-to-wall harmonizes with the brown and cream striped upholstery and the tan wall below the chair rail. The gray-blue upper wall is decorated with a pattern that seems to be stenciled rather than wallpaper since it does not repeat under the window. The drapes are a rich rose. The idea of painting the chair rail and the baseboard a brown instead of the tan of the lower wall and the door molding may well be unique as far as contemporary paintings reveal. The carpet in the back room is a greenish blue with a darker diamond pattern.

Of added interest are the family pets. Birds were widely popular in America from the very beginning, but the presence of two of them seems to indicate an especial interest by the Sargents. These are fairly big birds, but their yellow color suggests that they may have been intended for canaries. The playful little dog is at least part spaniel and may well have been as pure-bred a specimen as one could find in America at this date.

Plate 15. *Music Recital* by an unknown artist, watercolor, c. 1800. Collection of Edgar William and Bernice Chrysler Garbisch.

Some students have suggested that this interesting painting may be English, and there are elements that seem to support this origin. Nevertheless, the picture itself was discovered in New Hampshire in circumstances that suggest a good chance for an American provenance. Aside from a general feeling, perhaps the best reason for suggesting an English scene is the coal grate in the fireplace. Most Americans at this time burned wood. No matter what its origin, however, the floral wall-to-wall carpeting in reds and greens harmonizes with the light green walls and their floral borders. Once again the multiple pictures are clearly hung much higher than modern taste would indicate. The instrument shown is a double manual harpsichord, which again leads one to believe that this painting may be of English provenance.

Plate 16. *Nathan Hawley and Family* by William Wilkie, watercolor, November 3, 1801. By permission of Albany Institute of History and Art.

When William Wilkie painted this watercolor of Nathan Hawley and his family he was an inmate in the Albany County jail and Hawley, the jailer, lived next door. As a jailer, Hawley probably represented a man of moderate means, and this is reflected in the bare floor of the rear room and the modest painted floor cloth in what is very apparently the best room. The clothing, however, is in good style, and there are a number of pictures hung high on the wall with screw eyes and nails, a popular technique during the first quarter of the century. The windows are drapeless, but afford folding shutters for privacy.

NATHAN HAWLEY, and FAMILY, Nov.ʳ 3.ᵈ 1801.

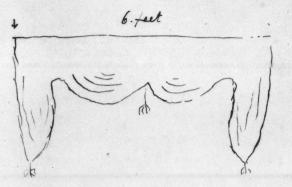

Plate 17. *Window Drapery for the Study at Monticello* by Thomas Jefferson, ink, March 2, 1808. The Library of Congress.

Interested in every phase of architecture and interior design, Thomas Jefferson drew a number of sketches between 1798 and 1808 for window drapes for his home at Monticello and for other dwellings. Four of these sketches survive in the Massachusetts Historical Society and the Library of Congress. The pattern shown here seems to have been the basic style preferred by the great statesman, but sometimes he combined it with a rectangular valance, a second and lower set of swags and festoons or with curtains. Usually he also added fringe as well as the tassels shown here. The description accompanying this sketch reads:

> Drapery for the tops of 4 windows (no curtains being desired) somewhat in the stile here drawn.—
> of common damask silk, lined with green and a yellow fringe.
> There are in the House of representatives 2 small prints with drapery in this style, which will give a just idea of what is desired, the architraves of the windows are exactly 6 feet from out to out. Th: Jefferson asks the favour of Mr. Rea to furnish him with the above at any time within the course of the present month.

John Rea replied with a more detailed drawing of this drapery, which he proceeded to furnish as requested.

Plate 18. "Christian Rupp and Kunkel, at the dinner Table, 1809," watercolor from Lewis Miller, *Sketches and Chronicles.* From the Collection of the Historical Society of York County in York, Pennsylvania.

Lewis Miller was a carpenter who closely observed life in his native York, and, in his old age, set out to chronicle and illustrate it. Here he portrays the setting for a family dinner of 1809, without spoons, which seems usually to have been the case. At the same time he indicates the use of Windsor chairs for eating and the employment of a dining table with a drawer.

Plate 19. *The Poor Author and the Rich Bookseller* by Washington Allston, oil, c. 1810. Courtesy, Museum of Fine Arts, Boston.

This represents an office rather than a home (though it may well have been in a home). Still, it illustrates a fine example of a hat and coat rack such as any home of the period might have offered in its hall. The great looking glass, the long cloth cover on the table, and the inkwell also apply to home decoration. And, besides, the subject is so elevating that it deserves inclusion in any compilation!

Plate 20. *Lolotte et Werther* by Eunice Pinney, watercolor, October 23, 1810. National Gallery of Art, Washington, D. C. Gift of Edgar William and Bernice Chrysler Garbisch.

The use of French for a picture title illustrating Goethe's *Sorrows of Young Werther* raises a number of interesting questions. Did Eunice Pinney of Connecticut read this popular work of 1774 in the original German, in English or perhaps in some French translation? Perhaps the use of another language in the title represents an attempt to suggest a romance in another land, and one wonders if some of the picture details also were intended to indicate a somewhat exotic room. The chair, indeed, seems a bit fanciful with a Windsor back and Hepplewhite legs and seat rail, but other details seem possible for America. The French doors without curtains or drapes are known in other pictures of American rooms, and the wall-to-wall carpeting or floor cloth is quite typical. For that matter, so is the print in its gilt frame hung by a single screw eye and nail. Nevertheless the very fact that this fine primitive watercolor was intended to illustrate an event in another land and at another time makes it a prime example of the type of picture that the student should ponder carefully before accepting it as evidence of contemporary American practices.

Eunice Finney, Drawing.   October the 23rd AD 1810.

LOLOTTE ET WERTHER.

Plate 21. *Family Group* by an unknown artist, oil, 1810–1815. Collection of Bertram K. and Nina Fletcher Little.

Like the portrait of the Sargent Family in plate 14, this informative painting offers a glimpse of the world of an upper middle class household, presumably in New England. Once again the family pets are much in evidence, this time a kitten and another reasonably pure-bred spaniel. The window draperies with the unusual valance featuring a central plaque and the fine ornamental tie-backs for the side pieces are exceptionally handsome. The hearth rug was one of the first separate throw rugs to appear in a principal room, and there is an excellent one in this picture. Presumably it protected the expensive carpet from stray sparks and also absorbed some of the wear from the feet of people who congregated in front of the fireplace. It is impossible to be sure, but this one appears to be a hooked rug, possibly made by the lady of the family. In this instance the screw eyes on the picture frames are used to hold a colored cord that passes over an ornamental hanger pin; and there are two distinctly different ways of tying the cords. Most unusual of all, however, is the presence of a small Hepplewhite sideboard, dimly seen against the wall at right, with a painted tin tray resting upon it. Normally these would be considered dining room furnishings, but the rest of the picture suggests a living room of a family prosperous enough to have had separate rooms for these purposes. The door at the left of the fireplace suggests by its location and separate keyhole that this anonymous family also possessed a closet, another unusual feature in a living room of that era!

Plate 22. *General Schumacker's Daughter* by Jacob Maentel, pen and watercolor, c. 1812. Collection of Edgar William and Bernice Chrysler Garbisch.

If this painting shows a typical room, General Schumacker of Pennsylvania maintained a simple home despite his rank and social position. The floor is bare of rug or floor cloth, and there are no drapes at the window. The walls, however, compensate for this lack of decoration with a stencil or stipple pattern below the chair rail, a two-color intertwined border above the rail and around the window and a floral swag border at the ceiling. Students of furniture may also ponder the bamboo-turned Windsor chair with 11 spindles at a time when 7 are thought to be good and 9 are considered a sign of excellence.

Plate 23. *Family Portrait* by Jacob Maentel, watercolor, 1810–1830. Courtesy the Henry Francis du Pont Winterthur Museum.

Jacob Maentel quite possibly painted this anonymous family in Pennsylvania as he had General Schumacker's daughter. Nothing is known about the subjects, but they seem to be solidly of the middle class, with a liking for bright colors and absolutely no concern about combining a number of different busy patterns in a small room. The blue floor covering with its red and yellow flowers is probably a painted floor cloth. The bamboo-turned chairs are yellow with red and green decorations, and there are still other colors and patterns on the walls above and below the chair rail. These, too, are quite probably stenciled rather than papered. Aside from the riot of colors and patterns, the most interesting feature of the painting is the fact that the fireplace has been closed with a two-piece fireboard for the summer to minimize the black emptiness that so evidently disturbed early Americans.

Plate 24. *Quilting Party* by John Lewis Krimmel, oil, 1813. Courtesy the Henry Francis du Pont Winterthur Museum.

A fine genre painter, Krimmel is noted among students of social history for his use and re-use of rooms and models. This particular painting is generally thought to represent the celebration of the completion of a quilt, but it has also been suggested that it depicts the traditional gift of a quilt to a newly-wed pair who stand at right. Krimmel used the same room, many of the same props (slightly rearranged) and some of the same models for his well-known *A Country Wedding* now in the Pennsylvania Academy of Fine Arts. Still it reflects many attitudes and practices of his day (along with many interesting objects). The bare floor, the difference in color of the wall above and below the chair rail, and the position of the fowling piece, hunting bag and powder horn hung above the door are quite typical. So are the arrangement of pictures over the fireplace and the crockery and glassware in the cupboard. The military panoply next to the chimney, and the grouping of objects on the floor which carry the eye around the composition may be dismissed as artificial, but the bird-cage alongside the magnificent Chippendale tall-case clock suggest the popularity of both these items in the early American home.

Plate 25. *The Toast* by an unknown artist, oil, 1810–1815. Courtesy the Bedford-Nugent Corporation.

This very English-looking scene of conviviality may possibly be American. Its discovery in this country and the wood of the stretchers at least suggest such a possibility. If it is indeed a native product, it offers an interesting comparison to the drawing of Peter Manigault and his friends shown in plate 4 and the musical evening of the *Friends and Amateurs of Musick* in Charlestown illustrated in plate 36. Here a group of gentlemen with long clay pipes and stemmed glasses gather around a table with a red cloth on which rests a Delft punch bowl, a crystal decanter, and an open snuff box. The floor is carpeted, suggesting a home rather than an inn, and pictures in gilt and gesso frames hang on concealed wires or strings. The inkwell and quill pens on the mantel offer further evidence that it may be a library or study. A double Argand chandelier provides light through which the man at the left enjoys the color of his wine and casts a yellow glow of bonhommie over the gathering. Perhaps the American and English all-male socials were not so different after all.

Plate 26. *Mrs. William Cooper* by Mrs. Freeman, watercolor, c. 1816. Courtesy New York State Historical Association.

When the unknown "Mrs. Freeman" recorded Elizabeth Fenimore Cooper she created a document unsurpassed in its illustration of interesting and unusual domestic details of the era. Otsego Hall stood near the shores of Lake Otsego, just outside Cooperstown, New York. Its inhabitants were a moderately wealthy country family with considerable mental independence and creativity. Elizabeth's husband, William Cooper, was an active politician and landowner and so belligerent that his fellow Quakers found it more comfortable without his membership in their Society. In 1809 this belligerence resulted in his death at the hands of another politician. Elizabeth's son, James Fenimore Cooper, became American's first major novelist. At the time this watercolor was painted he was living away from home, but he later returned and spent the remainder of his life in this gracious house. A later drawing of a room there during his occupancy is shown in plate 99.

In this picture Elizabeth sits in the center of the main hall which is carpeted wall-to-wall in what appears to be an ingrain carpet. It is summer, and the glass-beaded chandelier, hung on an iron rod, is covered with fine cloth in accord with custom. The great specially-made sofa "near twenty feet" long reflects the season in a light chintz slipcover. At the far end of the room rows of plants in wooden boxes flourish in light from the drapeless windows. Some, on the left, have strings for training their upward growth while a smaller plant in a double pot rests on a tall plant stand at the right.

Despite the fact that wallpaper had been popular in America for many years, this is one of the earliest pictures in which it can definitely be seen that the walls are papered rather than stenciled. From at least the middle of the 18th century the newspapers of major cities carried frequent advertisements for wallpaper. On January 19, 1765 John Blott maintained in *The South Carolina Gazette* that "The expense of papering a room does not amount to more than a middling set of Prints." On April 13, 1783 William Payntell advertised in the *Pennsylvania Journal* that he offered a selection of 4,000 pieces of wallpaper, some with flock patterns, and on August 16, with his stock reduced to 2,500 pieces he claimed that his low prices would "make papering cheaper than whitewashing," which seems hard to believe. Wallpaper was thus obviously a popular and inexpensive decorating medium even though it appears rarely in early pictures.

Plate 27. *Mrs. Denny Sockbasin* by an unknown artist, watercolor, September 18, 1817. Collection of Bertram K. and Nina Fletcher Little.

The full inscription beneath the painting informs us that Mrs. Sockbasin was the daughter of Francis Joseph [Neptune], Governor of the Passamaquoddy Indian Tribes, and that the picture was done at Eastport, Maine. The British officer and enlisted man seen through the window indicate that this was during the British occupation. The room in which Mrs. Sockbasin sits was apparently either in one of the barracks or officers' quarters. It is simple and severe. The bench is interesting as an early representation of an almost universal form with V-cut feet that appears in both civilian and military contexts into the present century. The table has an unusual center stretcher, and the window is completely devoid of drapes or curtains, as one would expect in such a building. The pitchers and plate are pewter, and so is the spouted canteen hung against the window molding. All is drab and plain, setting off Mrs. Sockbasin's colorful Indian costume and silver jewelry to great advantage.

Plate 28. *Departure for a Boarding School* engraved by Goodman & Piggot from a drawing by John L. Krimmel from the *Analectic Magazine,* 1820. Courtesy the New York State Library.

This pair of pictures by Krimmel is humorous and overdrawn, but it makes a point about contemporary ideas of high style. In this first picture the daughter takes leave of her suitor and family as the coachman waits to take her to school. The room is simple and multi-purpose with a slate, a small looking glass, an almanac and agricultural prints on the wall. Her father, seated at his desk, counts out his savings from a strongbox on the bare floor.

Plate 29. *Return from Boarding School* by John L. Krimmel from the *Analectic Magazine,* 1820. Courtesy the New York State Library.

In this picture everything is changed. All the family possessions have been moved to the left side of the room, and the right side has become elegant. A piano replaces the desk, and there is a handsome work table holding cosmetics. The almanac and agricultural prints have been superseded by a large looking glass, a peacock feather and fashion plates. A porcelain basket, a memorial obelisk and a fan have displaced the utilitarian lamp and pottery containers on the mantel, and a carpet covers the bare floor. There is even a birdcage with an occupant large enough to be a parrot. The contrast clearly indicates Krimmel's conception of the conspicuous signs of taste and affluence sought by rising members of society.

Plate 30. *The Dinner Party* by Henry Sargent, oil, c. 1820. Courtesy, Museum of Fine Arts, Boston; gift of Mrs. Horatio A. Lamb in memory of Mr. & Mrs. Winthrop Sargent.

Many students believe that this detailed picture represents a fine Federal Style dining room in Sargent's own Boston home. Be that as it may, it is filled with information. The gentlemen diners have reached the final stage of their meal and sit with their fruit knives and plates and small stemmed glasses for a dessert wine or brandy from one of the group of mixed decanters and bottles on the table. There is a cellarette near the table, but other wine bottles rest in a straw-filled box beneath the Sheraton sideboard while five additional decanters and a silver water pitcher sit upon its top. There is a single lighted candlestick on the table, but the two adjustable Argand chandeliers appear unlit and there is a suggestion of light coming from the windows. These windows, incidentally, have two different kinds of shutters: folding paneled shutters on the left and louvered shutters on the right, and there are fringed drapes hung on rods. The wall-to-wall carpeting has an added border that follows the contours of the room, and there is a special extra floor covering beneath the table and chairs to protect it. Other interesting details include the fact that the paintings are hung (quite high) on concealed wires, the tiny shaded lamp on the sideboard, and the French clock in its glass bell or "shade" on the mantel.

Plate 31. *The Tea Party* by Henry Sargent, oil, c. 1820. Courtesy, Museum of Fine Arts, Boston; gift of Mrs. Horatio A. Lamb in memory of Mr. & Mrs. Winthrop Sargent.

Again students feel that this gala scene may have occurred in Sargent's Boston home. In these rooms, however, the furniture and decorations are all of the newer Empire style derived from French sources. The furniture is ebonized with gilt areas and ormolu mounts. The elaborate drapes are looped over posts with ornamental ends, and there appear to be glass curtains as well. The Sheraton "tabernacle" looking glass between the windows represents almost the only Federal style element in view. Lighting is provided by double and triple candelabra on the mantel and on wall brackets. The urn and artificial flower bouquet in its glass shade on the mantel represents an early manifestation of this device, and once again the wall-to-wall carpeting with center panel and borders has been cut and fitted to the room contours.

Plate 32. *The Schuyler Family* by Ambrose Andrews, watercolor, 1824. Courtesy of the New-York Historical Society, New York City.

Ambrose Andrews was an itinerant artist who captured this likeness of the Schuyler family in their home at Schuylerville near Saratoga, New York. Second only to the family in importance is the handsome Hepplewhite harpsichord played by one of the daughters seated on a rare form of adjustable piano stool. Almost hidden underneath is a large all-American mongrel dog. Otherwise the house is remarkably plain for so substantial a family. The floors are carpeted, and the chairs are decorated, but perhaps because it was summertime there are no hangings at the windows. A wallpaper border a few inches below the ceiling can be glimpsed in the back room where a handsome pier glass tilts out above a drop-leaf table with a drawer. An Empire sewing box rests upon this table, apparently one of the usual leather-covered or japanned types with ormolu mounts and bear-paw feet. Thus the furniture is deceptively fine despite the plain impression created by the watercolor with its muted colors.

Plate 33. *Interior of the Moses Morse House, Loudon, New Hampshire* by Joseph Warren Leavitt, 1824. Collection of Bertram K. and Nina Fletcher Little.

From Joseph Leavitt's painting one would judge that either Moses Morse or his wife was especially fond of painted decorations. Every visible room boasts at least one and sometimes several different designs. Indeed, it almost seems as if the furniture has been largely omitted just to emphasize these embellishments. The principal room in the foreground displays the ever popular checkered floor, a swag and pendant border around the wall at the ceiling and a leaf border beneath it that also completely outlines every panel of wall above the chair rail. There is even an overmantel painting of a bird resting on a bough with the same leaf pattern as the inner border. The middle room seems to have a simpler border around all wall panels, but the far room offers an all-over stencil pattern.

In addition to the very busy stenciling there is also a subject of interest in the fireplace. The artist's treatment of the golden area that envelopes the andirons may be intended to represent a fire, and perhaps Mrs. Morse (?) sits sewing so close to it for warmth. Still, it might also indicate a decorative bundle of straw or sea wheat that tradition suggests early Americans sometimes placed in the dead fireplaces of the summer to mitigate their black emptiness.

Plate 34. *The Itinerant Artist* by Charles Bird King, oil, c. 1825. Courtesy New York State Historical Association.

In this slightly murky composition Charles Bird King has distorted the size of the front room and cluttered it with an improbable number of barrels, baskets and melons. Yet he shows a wealth of details that ring absolutely true. A cord across the fireplace holds towels to dry, and a ham hanging on the nearby door frame has been whittled by snackers. Other hams depend from the ceiling beams along with drying hides. In the bedroom through the door one can note the one-piece curtain hung from a slightly slack cord or wire, the dress on a peg above the head of the low post bed, and the mirror hung near the window for light. The dog, incidentally, looks very much like an English setter. As an artist himself, King has been especially careful in depicting the painting gear used by the traveling portraitist, including the box of paints and brushes, the equipment for grinding pigments, the modeling stand, placed on two logs, even the improvised easel. The quaintness must be discounted, but the details are fine.

Plate 35. *Birth and Baptismal Certificate of Margaret Münch* by Carl E. Münch, watercolor, 1826. National Gallery of Art, Washington, D. C.; Gift of Edgar William and Bernice Chrysler Garbisch.

In the lower right hand corner of this informative document Carl Münch has suggested the multiple uses to which most rooms in the simpler American homes of the early 19th century were put. Here one woman prepares food at a table while another spins. A gentleman sits behind an iron stove while another pets the family dog. And the cat relaxes completely by itself. Except for a handsome tall-case clock in the Germanic manner and the fine stove, the room is plain with bare floor, drapeless window and undecorated walls, just as one might expect of such a home in Northumberland County, Pennsylvania.

Margareta Münch

Ist geboren den 8ten December im Jahr 1808.
in Freyburg, Penns Township, Northumberland County
im Staat Pennsylvania. Die Eltern sind: Carl E.
Münch und Anna Margareta, geborne Bieser. Ihre
Tauf-Zeuge war: Elisabeth Heffer, Weib von John
Heffer. Sie wurde von Hr. Adam getauft, und
vom Ehrw: Isaac Gerhart, ref. Pred. in der
Hoffmans Kirche den 13ten
May   im Jahr 1826.
confirmirt.

Plate 36. *Friends and Amateurs of Musick* by Thomas Middleton, wash drawing, 1827. Courtesy of the Carolina Art Association, Charleston.

Despite the fact that this delightful picture has suffered over the years, it still echoes with the gaiety of a convivial gathering of musically inclined Charlestonians who congregated "to beguile away the time in listening to the soothing strains of their own music" as the artist described it. And he added, "I have to apologize for certain glass . . . on the table, but it was Vain to remonstrate." The gentleman at the right, in fact, seems to have succumbed to the glasses and the gaiety sufficiently to be inspired to attempt to play the case for his cello. Thomas Middleton himself stands at center with his flute. Otherwise one may note the strategically placed (though small) cuspidors and the arrangement of the pictures on the walls. Not only are they hung above eye-level with blind cords, but over the mantel one painting actually overlaps another. The floor is absolutely plain, which may well indicate either a straw or canvas covering or a lapse on the part of the artist in failing to indicate details.

Plate 37. *Charles Carroll of Carrollton* by Thomas Sully, watercolor, 1829. Walters Art Gallery, Baltimore.

This sketch by Sully and the following oil painting by William James Hubbard offer an interesting contrast, both in man and room. Here the great Maryland statesman sits in a mid 18th century chair next to a Chinese Chippendale table of the same vintage. The floor covering, perhaps a single color canvas, seems to cover the entire floor area in typical period fashion. Most spectacular is the big Chinese screen that acts as a partial room divider (and as an artistic device as well). Such screens are known to have been in use through inventories and other records, but they rarely appear in contemporary pictures. One other painting that shows such a screen a decade later (and also in Maryland) is *Domestic Scene* painted about 1839 by James G. Sawkins. This painting was photographed for the J. Hall Pleasants File at the Maryland Historical Society many years ago, but its present location is unknown.

Plate 38. *Charles Carroll of Carrollton* by William James Hubbard, oil, 1830. The Metropolitan Museum of Art, Rogers Fund, 1956.

Painted just a year after the Sully sketch, this fine picture by the youthful Hubbard presents the 93-year-old Carroll in quite a different setting. The table may actually be the same one recorded by Sully, but here it is covered with a floor-length fringed cloth. The chair, too, may possibly be the same, though the arm supports seem to be straighter and there is just the suggestion of a cabriole leg beneath the slipcover. This slipcover, in fact, is one of the most important aspects of the portrait from the standpoint of interior decoration. It leaves the arms bare but covers the back and seat and stretches clear to the floor without pattern, ruffle or fringe. Were it not for the fact that Carroll is obviously using it for his reading and writing, one might almost mistake it for a dustcover, though here again the bare arms would negate that identification. The crucifix in the upper left corner may have actually stood in the room, but more likely it is a symbol of Carroll's devout Roman Catholicism just as the wintry picture opposite suggests his old age. The floor covering, incidentally, seems to be the same plain, neutral-colored floor cloth that Sully suggested.

Plate 39. *A Bedroom Interior* by an unknown artist, pencil, c. 1830. Courtesy the Cooper-Hewitt Museum of Design, Smithsonian Institution.

It is highly problematical whether the furniture shown in this drawing was ever built. There are no known comparable pieces in public or private collections today. There are features in the designs, however, that presage developments that did occur 70 to 100 years later.

Plate 40. *The Talcott Family* by Deborah Goldsmith, watercolor, 1832. Abby Aldrich Rockefeller Folk Art Collection, Williamsburg, Virginia.

The arrangement of the painted fancy chairs suggests that they have been pulled together to hold the family for their portraits, but the rest of the Talcotts' living room is quite evidently real. The walls are either papered or stenciled above the baseboard, and the floor is covered with a typical Venetian carpet. No one knows quite how the carpeting came to be called Venetian, but it was a striped non-pile floor covering that became popular in America about 1800 and continued in use well into the present century as an inexpensive machine-made carpet. Usually it was striped as shown here, but there are references indicating that sometimes it came in a checked pattern as well. The drapes appear to be simple white muslin, and the massive Sheraton cupboard may well have been the outstanding piece of furniture in the room. It seems unlikely that the family dog had quite the chihuahua proportions indicated, but at least he must have been small and welcomed as an indoor pet.

Plate 41. *Self Portrait with the Ward Family* by Ann Hall, oil, c. 1834. Courtesy Kennedy Galleries, Inc., New York City.

If Ann Hall's depiction of the Ward home is accurate, it was a well-to-do and·cultured menage. At least the piano, the books, the globe and the quality of the furnishings would suggest this. The floor is shown with a black and white checkered pattern similar to that encountered in pictures of American homes from the mid 17th century on. By this date, however, it was probably composed of the actual squares of black and white marble that the earlier floor cloths were meant to simulate. This theory is reinforced by the fringed carpet that covers the floor in the center of the room. Such a carpet would hardly have been used to cover an inexpensive floor cloth, but it would have warmed and softened a marble paving. On the far wall a fine bombé chest of drawers associates with the later piano and the very modern chairs. The paintings and the statuette on the bracket are exceptionally high on the wall though the ornate clock is hung at a better viewing height. The window is bare of hangings, and the drape at the left must be considered as artistic license, not a feature of the real room. The family dog seems to be at least part and possibly pure English setter, the second earliest positively identifiable breed in American paintings.

Plate 42. *Joseph Emery. Aged 25 & 2 months, 1834, Sarah Ann Emery. Aged 20 years, 1834* by Joseph H. Davis, watercolor. Courtesy the New York State Historical Association.

All of the furnishings and accessories in this portrait watercolor may well be imaginary. Still, the objects shown document several preferences and practices of the period. The picture on the wall is hung on nails by two screw eyes in the usual fashion; the table, on the other hand, is marbleized in bright colors quite different from the usual technique, which attempted to imitate nature. The flower arrangement is perhaps the most interesting aspect of the scene. Identifiable flowers include the ever popular roses, morning glories—which early Americans regarded more highly than their modern descendants—bachelor's buttons, and other less recognizable varieties. The unrealistic combination of flowers and dried plant materials from all seasons suggests that this is a Bouquet of Eternity, with obvious symbolic meaning.

Joseph Emery.   AGED, 25   *Sarah Ann Emery.*   AGED-
                                  & 2 months.   20 years.
                                       1834   -1834-

Plate 43.   *Mary D. Varney. Born December 20th 1814. Painted at the Age of 21. 1835* by Joseph II. Davis, watercolor. Courtesy the New York State Historical Association.

In this very typical Davis painting the significant item is the flower pot, apparently made of pottery, which sits upon a dirt-filled basin of the same material. It might be drawing a long bow to deduce from so artificial a composition that bushes growing in such pots were to be found inside on expensive carpets, but other more literal pictures support that assumption. From at least 1800 on American families sought to bring color and greenery inside, until, by 1870, some rooms became almost jungles of vines and plants.

Plate 44. *Interior, Man Facing Woman* by Joseph H. Davis, watercolor, c. 1835. Abby Aldrich Rockefeller Folk Art Collection, Williamsburg, Virginia.

Another very typical Davis painting of a well-to-do young couple. The striking carpet patterns undoubtedly came directly from the artist's imagination as did the gaily "marbleized" furniture. One must assume, however, that such furniture would have been acceptable to the subjects and not completely out of keeping with their style of living. The accessories quite probably relate directly to the subjects since these vary considerably from picture to picture. Here the combination of books, inkwell, pens and paper plus the man's clothes strongly suggest that he was a lawyer. The cat is quite probably a favorite family pet.

Plate 45. *Young Woman of Faul Family, Age 21 Years* by Jacob Maentel, water-color, c. 1835. Collection of Edgar William and Bernice Chrysler Garbisch.

Even in so restricted a composition, Jacob Maentel has offered several useful bits of information about this Pennsylvania room. The window boasts drapes which seem to be nailed to the top of the molding, and behind them are glass curtains of lace with rows of tiny tassels along their inner edges. The walls are painted the same color both above and below the chair rail, which can be seen at window sill level just above the top of the drop-leaf table. In her hand Miss Faul holds a rose, by far the most popular flower among Americans of the 18th and 19th century, and she stands on a carpet that does not cover the floor wall-to-wall in the earlier fashion but exposes a narrow border of dark painted wood.

Plate 46. *Sportsman with Dog* by an unknown artist, oil, c. 1835. Abby Aldrich Rockefeller Folk Art Collection, Williamsburg, Virginia.

The method of hanging a gun in a period room has long been a subject of discussion among museum people and collectors. Most realize that firearms seldom actually hung above the fireplace in the traditional manner, but at that point unanimity stops. This handsome portrait illustrates the use of straps to support a double-barreled shotgun upside down on a wall, a technique which appears in other pictures as well. The powder flask and shot belt hang with it. A single-barreled fowler stands in the corner behind the curly maple chair. Other points of interest include the sporting print or painting again hung by nails and screw eyes in the top of the frame and the solid color tablecloth with an added border of what may be silk, satin or even velvet. The dog seems to be a well-bred pointer more than coincidentally duplicating the one in the picture on the wall.

Plate 47. *The Sportsman's Last Visit* by William Sidney Mount, oil, 1835. Suffolk Museum & Carriage House, Stony Brook, Long Island.

In this magnificent rendering of a simple domestic interior Mount portrays a host of interesting details of decorative practices. The ceiling beams stand revealed, and the floor is bare except for the hearth rug, though the successful suitor sits on a decorated arrow-back chair with bamboo-turned legs. The drape at the window is tacked to the molding and pulled to one side, and there is a potted plant on the sill. One of the problems that has long puzzled students of American life has been the method of storing fuel handily. Here it seems to have been laid on the hearth as the log in the lower right corner suggests. On the wall there is a framed floral print hung over a nail with an exposed cord, a kerchief and hat hung on pegs in a board, and a sickle over a nail. The walls themselves apparently are whitewashed, and a special detail of interest is the pot-holder hung on a nail from the mantel face.

Plate 48. *Mount Family Kitchen* by William Sidney Mount, pencil, 1830–1840. Suffolk Museum & Carriage House, Stony Brook, Long Island.

A careful recorder of any milieu that might possibly serve as a setting for a painting, Mount sketched many homely details of American life. In this very accurate sketch he portrays a middle class kitchen of the 1830's. Students of furniture styles will immediately notice that he has combined an early gateleg table and ladderback chair with a much more "modern" decorated Windsor that must have been quite new when the sketch was made. Even more significant is the paucity of cooking utensils around the fireplace. The hearth supports only a teakettle, a grill and tongs. There is none of the crowded array associated with most refurnished kitchens, an array which would surely have tripped a cook trying to work there. Another very sensible feature is the variety of hooks on the crane which would have made it practical to shift a kettle to almost any desired height for controlling the temperature of its contents. Quite to be expected also are the bare floor and the curtainless window.

Plate 49. *Front chamber of house No. 42 South 8th Street. Residence of J. S. Russell in 1835* by Joseph Shoemaker Russell, watercolor. Collection of Bertram K. and Nina Fletcher Little.

Apparently no one lived in the front room of Mr. Russell's Philadelphia home when he decided to record it for posterity. It is completely devoid of any sign of human personality. Except for a pitcher and bowl the washstands and dresser are bare, and no ornaments grace the mantel. The shutters on two of the front windows are closed while the equally drapeless third one discloses the front of the house across the street. Three side chairs seem a bit much for a bedroom, and the floor is carpeted in the wall-to-wall manner, an unusual luxury for even a front chamber. Other items of unusual interest include the very high fender before the fireplace and the fine big cupboard which offers a door in the side as well as the double doors between the pilasters on the front. It may be that this painting is misdated since the other room portraits by Mr. Russell (illustrated in plates 91 to 95) are all dated 1853 and 1854. These later pictures depict his living conditions in a boarding house where there is every evidence of human use and activity, however, and so it is likely that the similarity of the numbers is just a coincidence.

Front chamber of house No

outh 8ᵗʰ Street. Residence of J.S. Russell in   1835

Plate 50.   *Bishop White's Study* by John Sartain, oil, 1836. Independence National Historical Park. A mezzotint by the same artist based on his oil painting appeared in Bird, Wilson, *Memoir of the Life of the Right Reverend William White, D.D.,* Philadelphia 1839. It shows some details more clearly.

William White, first Protestant Episcopal bishop of the diocese of Pennsylvania, died in his Philadelphia home early in the summer of 1836. Within a few weeks John Sartain appeared upon the scene to paint a portrait of the study in which the scholarly bishop had worked. It was an eclectic room where late dark green "Sheraton" Windsor chairs with bamboo turnings sat next to fine Chippendale side chairs and a handsome earlier Windsor chair with mahogany arms. The loose green cushion in this chair is especially interesting for it documents a practice that many decorators have thought to be modern. This one is even tied in place with tapes. There is a coal grate in the fireplace. Notes and a candle clutter the mantel, while a pair of scissors hangs from the chair rail, ready to hand. This was a fine city house, and the fireplace is faced with real Pennsylvania marble instead of the marbleized wood often encountered in this period. The walls are white, probably indicating that they were whitewashed or covered with a water soluble mixture of white lead, a much more practical paint that has been found on the walls of some houses in this area.

Since this was summer, the carpets have been taken up and replaced by straw matting in both the study and the bedroom which can be glimpsed through the door. This Canton or Madras matting, as it was often called, was popular as a summer floor covering from at least the 1770's on. It should be noted, however, that Joshua Brooks found the floor of the banqueting room at Mount Vernon covered with straw matting in January when he visited Washington in the winter of 1798, while Thomas Jefferson is said to have used the matting as a "crumb catcher" in the White House dining room during his two terms of office. The summer season may also account for the lack of drapes on the bedroom windows, though window hangings were by no means universal even for wealthy and sophisticated people at this time.

Plate 51. *The Pedlar Displaying His Wares* by Asher Durand, oil, c. 1836. Courtesy the New-York Historical Society, New York City.

Asher Durand painted a great many genre scenes during the second quarter of the 19th century. Unfortunately, his credibility quotient is low. Furniture is introduced and objects arranged primarily for pictorial reasons. His pictures thus

make excellent examples of the type of contemporary paintings that cannot be accepted as documents for a study such as this. In this scene however, there is one fascinating feature in the shelf hung from the ceiling beams. Presumably even Durand would not have made up something that was absolutely unthinkable, and so it is quite possible that such shelves did exist even though no other picture has yet been found to confirm them.

Plate 52. *General Stephen Van Rensselaer* attributed to Chester Harding, oil, c. 1838. Courtesy the New-York Historical Society, New York City.

General Van Rensselaer died in 1839 at the age of 75, and so this portrait must have been painted at almost the end of his life. It shows him in the library of a substantial New York home. One of his slipper-clad feet rests upon a foot cushion rarely depicted in American paintings. More unusual still is the set of library steps in the lower left-hand corner, for these are usually considered an English accessory. And these steps are covered with a carpet runner, perhaps to protect their surfaces, perhaps to make them less slippery. Otherwise the room is fairly typical. The classical bust on its marble pedestal rests in a niche between two glass-fronted bookcases with drawers and cupboards below. One pedestal table is bare, the other covered with a long cloth that dips almost to the carpeted floor in places. The draped portrait leaning against the table is quite probably an artistic device to recall a departed forebear.

Plate 53. *John Thomas Avery, Aged 11. Painted 1839* by an unknown artist, water-color. Collection of Mr. and Mrs. Samuel Schwartz.

The scatter rugs so popular in "early American" rooms today are rarely seen in contemporary pictures. From the painting one may guess that these shown here are hooked rugs with yellow and orange designs on a black background. At least the front one is fringed. The stenciled walls with designs in a light reddish brown document the persistence of an earlier style.

Plate 54. Frontispiece from *The Well Bred Boy* . . . , Boston, 1839. Society for the Preservation of New England Antiquities.

The well-bred boy in this woodcut is probably just as fictitious as his room. It is highly unlikely that either ever existed. Still, the artist has included a number of especially interesting details as well as showing what an ideal boy's room might have looked like. Most unusual for a boy of such tender years is the cuspidor beside his chair, and it makes one wonder if he could possibly have been chewing tobacco at his age. The bed hangings are less a cause of speculation, but they are highly instructive, as is the method of making the bed with the pillow exposed and the sheet turned down over the quilted comforter. There is even a throw rug beside the bed laid over the room carpet. The pictures are quite obviously unframed and just as obviously tacked to the wall. The window drapes boast a ruffled valance and the side panels are tucked up over a tie-back. But the feature that leaves the viewer with a final touch of wonderment is the light colored cloth covering the work table. Were well-bred boys of 1839 that careful with their pens and ink?

Plate 55. *The Muse—Susan Walker Morse* by Samuel F. B. Morse, oil, c. 1835–1837. The Metropolitan Museum of Art; bequest of Herbert L. Pratt, 1945.

The background of Morse's magnificent portrait of Susan is entirely imaginary, but the father of the telegraph has left one of the very best illustrations of the design of slipcovers and cushions of the late 1830's and 1840's. He leaves no detail of the construction of these decorative accessories to the imagination. One can note the seams, the silk or satin borders, the fringe, and the tassel in his fine representation of the divan on which Susan sits and sketches. The tiny footstool with its damask cover, however, is a rare type, if indeed it actually ever existed.

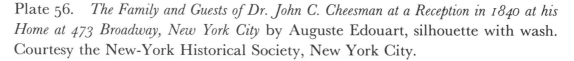

Plate 56. *The Family and Guests of Dr. John C. Cheesman at a Reception in 1840 at his Home at 473 Broadway, New York City* by Auguste Edouart, silhouette with wash. Courtesy the New-York Historical Society, New York City.

Silhouettes are usually simple portraits, but this fine one offers a masterpiece of detail. Behind the three standing gentlemen at the left is a divan slipcovered much in the same manner as that in the portrait of Susan Walker Morse (plate 55). Its upholstery matches that on the two sofas and the bench against the back wall. The floor is covered with wall-to-wall carpeting, but there is also a separate

hearth rug for extra protection. The fireplace itself is decorated for summertime with a fire board, and the mantel boasts elaborate candelabra (without candles) and a bird on a branch in a glass shade. The draperies are exceptionally elegant with the huge swags and the opaque drapes drawn to the outsides of the pair of windows, while the glass curtains are drawn to the insides. The tie-backs for the glass curtains are clearly shown. There are probably similar tie-backs for the drapes, but they are concealed. The great pier mirror is there also but easily missed in the magnificence of the hangings.

Plate 57. *Country Life, Penn^a. 1840* attributed to August Kollner, watercolor. The Chicago Historical Society.

In the lower left corner of this stark interior, the artist noted that the time was "before Breakfast." The bare wooden walls and floor, and the curtainless window were typical of simple homes throughout the country. The rocking chair and the sideboard show surprising quality when compared with the table and straight chair, thus attesting to the fallacy of those restorers who insist upon a common quality and period for all the furniture for their refurnished rooms. The shelf above the door holding pitchers and crocks is an interesting detail, and the gun in the chimney corner is the closest that any contemporary picture yet found has placed a firearm to a fireplace. Finally, the painting documents the belief that the Pennsylvania Dutch tradition of building a fire without andirons continued even at this date.

try life, Penn.ª 1840.   *Lebe´ i´m´ Lande´ morgens´.*

Plate 58. *Family Group* by Frederick R. Spencer, oil, 1840. In the Brooklyn Museum Collection.

Unnamed but obviously young and prosperous, this family group pose proudly in their stylish home. The dark walls reflect the change from the lighter tones that had been popular for a century, and the wall-to-wall carpeting is also dark, as are the drapes. The Empire sofa is not slipcovered, but it boasts an interesting ruffled skirt with a fringe. For flower interest one can note the climbing roses outside the window and the very typical arrangement in the vase on the marble-topped table with roses, a peony, possibly honeysuckle and other summer flowers.

Plate 59. *Rosa Heywood* by an unknown artist, oil, c. 1840. Abby Aldrich Rocke-feller Folk Art Collection, Williamsburg, Virginia.

The rose in the hand of this charming young lady may well be a symbol for her name, and so may be the rosebush growing in the planter in the background. It does seem odd to find such a bush growing indoors against an interior wall. Yet the fact that an indoor rosebush was not considered outrageous is suggestive, and the wooden planter on a pedestal is a fascinating design. Otherwise, one may note the figured green wallpaper above the chair rail and the plain matching green below, as well as the matching carpet with its big bordered figures on a floral background. They are not so extreme as those depicted by Joseph H. Davis (plates 42 to 44), but they do indicate that his conceptions were not entirely imaginary.

Plate 6o. *Rebecca Jaques, aged 79 Years, painted in the Year 1841* by Jacob Maentel, watercolor. Abby Aldrich Rockefeller Folk Art Collection, Williamsburg, Virginia.

In this portrait of a grand old dame, Jacob Maentel notes in the open Bible that earthly homes are transient while spiritual homes are eternal. Still, he offers some interesting insights into the earthly variety. The floor covering in a tartan check is evidently a painted floor cloth, and the walls are stenciled in blue both above and below the pink chair rail. The red drapes are thin and simple. Quite probably they were nailed at the top of the window and again at the point of tie-back. The green bamboo-turned Windsor chair is also interesting if it is exactly portrayed, for it is a left-handed writing-arm Windsor, an aberration that has not survived in any known specimen.

Plate 61. *Group Silhouette* by Auguste Edouart, silhouette with wash background, 1842. Courtesy the Henry Francis du Pont Winterthur Museum.

The date written on the silhouette is somewhat suspect, but the period is absolutely correct. Here Edouart shows another elegant drawing room with especially complicated drapes and curtains. There seem to be three different fabrics involved in the treatment that combines the two windows and the pier mirror between them as a single unit. First are the outer drapes that hang in big swags and festoons. These drapes are fringed, and there is a gold (?) rope with tassel for accent. Beneath these drapes are others of an apparently lighter material, long on the outer edges and short on the inner edges where they are held by flower-shaped tie-backs. Finally there are lace glass curtains held back on the inner edges by stamped ormolu tie-backs. The pier table beneath the mirror supports an astral lamp on its top and a collection of seashells on its lower shelf. The sofa is graced with another of the thin rectangular cushions that had largely supplanted the cylindrical type popular in the earlier Empire period. The carpet, even in so opulent a room, is not wall-to-wall at this date.

Plate 62. *The Yankee Pedlar* by an unknown artist, oil, 1840–1845. Collection of the IBM Corporation.

Far more precise than Asher Durand's earlier painting of a peddler (plate 51), this American primitive slyly suggests both the peddler's salesmanship and the housewife's scepticism. It also depicts the first specific indication of the so-called cottage curtains across the lower window sash. The high shelf above the window confirms a continuing practice while the wag-on-the-wall clock and the deer skull above the door are both instructive. One wonders if the hesitant dog at the door belongs to the peddler or just happened to investigate the open portal.

Plate 63. *Ideal Interior* by Andrew Jackson Davis, watercolor, 1845. Courtesy the New-York Historical Society, New York City.

There is no evidence that Davis' plan ever developed into an actual room though it does greatly resemble the great Merchant's House in New York. Still, it suggests an ideal blend of classically inspired architecture and furniture. The columns, friezes and moldings are complemented by the klismos type chairs and the classic designs on the sofa, divan, lamps and fire screen. The floor may be either carpeted or decorated with a mosaic, but it is difficult to tell from the painting.

Plate 64. *Jane Rebecca Griffith* attributed to Oliver T. Eddy, oil, c. 1840. From the collections of the Maryland Historical Society.

The Griffith home as depicted by Eddy comes as close as any to reflecting the ideal of Andrew Jackson Davis shown in the preceding plate. The friezes are lacking, but the moldings are classical, and the Corinthian columns are clearly visible. The furniture is quite different from the forms that Davis suggested. They are in the late Empire or "Restauration" style, and they relate more to the geometric carpet pattern than to the architecture. The two thin cushions laid flat on the sofa are an interesting and unusual detail.

Plate 65. *Family of Joseph Moore* by Erastus Salisbury Field, oil, c. 1840. Courtesy, Museum of Fine Arts, Boston, M. & M. Karolik Collection.

Mr. and Mrs. Moore sit on Hitchcock chairs on a yellow carpet that must have been a great trial to keep clean. A small work table holds a thread stand and serves in lieu of a pier table beneath the pier glass. The windows are curtainless, and the drapes are quite probably imaginary—or at least exaggerated for artistic effect. As is so often the case in contemporary pictures, the shutters on the outside of the windows are closed.

Plate 66. *Schuyler Ogden and his Sister* by George Harvey, oil, 1842. Courtesy Kennedy Galleries, Inc., New York City.

"The Hall," according to the *American Agriculturist,* "is generally a mere passage-way to something better beyond, and therefore it should not be so embellished as to attract special notice." This flat statement appeared in the December 1866 issue of the famous rural newspaper, but it expressed a philosophy that had long been in vogue, and, ironically, was then actually in the process of changing. Still, this charming portrait of the grandchildren of General Stephen Van Rensselaer (plate 52) in their Hudson Valley home shows a number of interesting details of decoration. Most obvious is the marble floor in a widely popular pattern of the period. Less visible, but more important, is the striped or Venetian stair carpet held in place by rods. This is an early date for such a feature. Finally, there is the door painted in two colors, neither of which appear to match the color of the moldings.

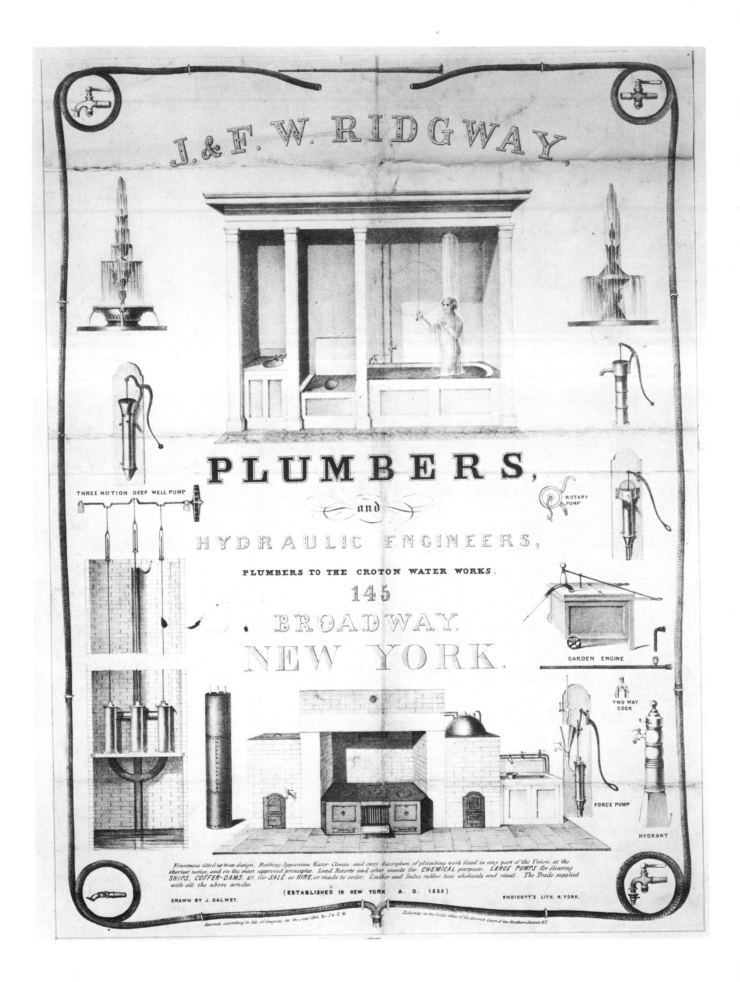

Plate 67. *Plumbing Advertisement for J. & F. W. Ridgway,* lithograph, 1844. The Library of Congress.

In the early 1840's New York City began piping water from the Croton River, and soon plumbers such as the Ridgways were offering all sorts of conveniences including tubs with showers, sinks and water closets. This was by no means the first appearance of such sybaritic luxuries in America. As early as 1810 the Markoe House, a Philadelphia hotel, offered most of them to its guests. Still, it was early for average city people to have such options. In the 1850's Robert E. Lee designed and installed inside plumbing in the Custis-Lee Mansion at Arlington as a personal innovation. And Pauline Dakin Taft related in *The Happy Valley* that at her family's country home, "Woodbine," in Cherry Valley, New York: "In 1860 they had installed the first bathroom in town. Lenny's brother Paul, at eighty-four recalled: 'I, as a little boy, was not encouraged to use it. In fact, it was generally reserved for emergencies.' Ample provision for a large family was made elsewhere, a room behind the summer kitchen for the women and children and an outhouse beyond the woodshed for the men, trellised over with woodbine. Since the ladies made a social affair of the morning visit there and generally went in a group with the children, one can readily understand why provision was made for so many at once."

Plate 68. *Plumbing Advertisement for Thomas Dusenbury,* lithograph, c. 1843–1845. J. Clarence Davies Collection, Museum of the City of New York.

Thomas Dusenbury also advertised running water from the Croton River, but his conceptual bathroom was even fancier than that of his competitors with curtains and tie-backs and even an American eagle for a finial. The dual faucets suggest that he, too, like the Ridgways, envisioned a stove in the basement to heat the water. In one aspect, however, he had a distinct advantage over his rival firm. Water Street is an infinitely more appropriate address for a plumber than Broadway could ever be!

THOMAS DUSENBURY, PLUMBER,
269 WATER STREET,
NEAR PECK SLIP,
N.Y.

CROTON WATER.

Plate 69. *Rubens Peale in His Studio* by Mary Jane Peale, oil, c. 1845. Courtesy Kennedy Galleries, Inc., New York City.

Mary Jane Peale used a very soft focus in her delineation of her father practicing the painting hobby that he took up late in life. Still, it is possible to note a number of interesting practices. It is a simple room with a bare floor and garments hanging openly on the wall. Yet the window has both drapes and glass curtains, both of which go all the way to the floor, and there is a good breakfront holding shelves of books and an oil lamp. The paintings are hung almost low enough to suit modern taste, and the small table with its long cloth, two candles and what seems to be a Bible suggests a family shrine. In the next room a stove sits on a metal plate designed to protect the floor from glowing coals. Curiously, it seems to sit directly in front of a bed or settee, and the stove pipe rises vertically before making the inevitable turn towards the wall and a chimney. On the windowsill is a large growing plant in a flowerpot. There appears to be a wall bracket placed very low just to the left of the breakfront. If so, it is empty, but the softness of Mary Peale's focus leaves this feature in eternal doubt.

Plate 70. *Rev. John Atwood and His family* by Henry F. Darby, oil, 1845. Courtesy, Museum of Fine Arts, Boston.

While the exact date of Henry Darby's birth is not known, he must have been a very young man when he painted this informative picture, if the date on the canvas is correct. Still, the costume, furniture and decorative practices illustrated all conform to this period. Most interesting of these is the fire board used to fill the fireplace for summer. It is covered with the same wallpaper that adorns the walls of the room. The fact that it is early summer is further attested by the bouquet in the tall vase on the mantel which contains pansies and other early-blooming flowers. Like some other American families of the period the Atwoods apparently had no worries about mixing a variety of busy patterns in one room. The walls, the borders, the tablecloth, and the carpet are all patterned. The drapes, however, are plain and hung with gathers on a rod. The pictures and mirror have spartanly simple frames, and the former are hung high on the wall with blind cords that allow them to tilt forward at a slight angle. The exceptionally handsome astral lamp with its brass column and marble base rests on a doily that appears to be crocheted rather than the usual piece of linen or lace. All in all, it is a room which suggests that the Atwoods enjoyed very comfortable circumstances.

Plate 71. *Mr. & Mrs. Charles Henry Augustus Carter,* attributed to Nicholas Biddle Kittell, oil, c. 1845. Museum of the City of New York.

A young New York City couple, the Carters had furnished their home in a mixture of Restauration and early Victorian furniture. The portraits are hung high on the darkish green walls with exposed cords that go up to the ceiling molding. The blue drapes are attached by rings to a rod and caught with tie-backs of yellow. Two gold ropes with tassels depend from the center. The combination of blues and greens is also noticeable in the short tablecloth with its darker border and the blue upholstery on the furniture. The lamp sits on a square doily, and the tiny bouquet represents a feature that became increasingly popular in the middle years of the century.

Plate 72. *Philip M. Beekman* by Auguste Edouart, silhouette with pencil background, 1846. Courtesy the New-York Historical Society, New York City.

Edouart made this silhouette of the short-lived Philip Beekman at Saratoga, New York. It is mainly noteworthy in the interior decoration field for its clear rendition of the use of glass curtains for one side of a window with a heavy drape for the swag, cascades and panel on the opposite side.

Plate 73. *Victorian Family* by an unknown artist, oil, c. 1845. Courtesy New York State Historical Association.

It is quite possible that the limner who painted this stiff group used stock figures to complete the more carefully delineated faces. If so, the background may also be completely fictitious. Still, he would not have shown details that would have been unacceptable to his customers, and so one may note this very late appearance of the black and white checkered floor. In a rural house this would still probably have been a painted floor cloth rather than the actual marble found at this date in more sophisticated homes. The tall vase rests on a square doily, and the principal flowers seem to be dahlias which were so popular at this period that visiting dignitaries were sometimes presented with garlands of them in civic ceremonies.

Plate 74. *A Greek Revival House Exterior* by Luther Briggs, Jr., wash drawing, 1845–1850. Society for the Preservation of New England Antiquities.

True, this is an exterior rather than an interior, but it offers excellent documentation of the techniques for draping windows among other things. All the windows on the ground floor have the drapes pulled to the left (or right if one regarded them from inside). They are fringed with tiny balls, and there is a broad fringe of the same style at the tops. In this case, both upper and lower floor drapes match, though the upper window drapes are bilaterally symmetrical rather than one-sided like those on the lower floor. Another feature of interest is the potted plant in the window next to the door.

Plate 75. *Soldier's Experience* by Richard Caton Woodville, wash drawing, March 1844. Courtesy the Walters Art Gallery.

For his first version of this discussion between the young soldier and the Revolutionary War veteran, Woodville selected a simple interior. The floor is bare, and the furnishings plain. The iron stove sits in a box of sand to protect the floor and the supply of firewood is stacked underneath. Especially interesting are the loose back cushion in the ladderback chair of the veteran and the slipcover over the seat with skirts that reach to the floor. Another unusual feature is the tacking of a print to the cupboard door. An early 18th century musket hangs upside down on pegs with a civilian-pattern tricorne hat, both relics of the past. The hats and coats of the present are hung on the wall just to the right of the cupboard where they are much more convenient for use.

Plate 76. *Old '76 and Young '48* by Richard Caton Woodville, oil, 1849. Courtesy the Walters Art Gallery.

Five years after his watercolor, Woodville redid his scene of a young soldier recounting his experiences to an elderly veteran. This time he selected a much more elegant setting for the conversation. The floor is carpeted with an Oriental rug, and a fringed fur hearth rug lies before the marble fireplace. On the mantelpiece are a fine clock, vases holding spills, candlesticks that have been converted into lamps with unusual shades, and, among other things, an ear of Indian corn! The walls are papered. The old musket has disappeared, but the tricorne hangs on the chimney breast next to the framed engraving. The table is set with silver and fine glass and boasts a handsome patterned tablecloth. Even the dog is better. He is still a pointer but more finely bred.

Plate 77. Woodcut by Theodore Boyd from *A Visit from St. Nicholas* by Clement C. Moore, New York, 1849.

"The children were nestled all snug in their beds. . . ." according to Moore before St. Nicholas made his appearance. Here Theodore Boyd illustrated the scene in one of the early editions of this classic. The children are in a trundle bed while the parents lie in a low post bed that is draped in the same fashion as the sleigh beds of the period. As far as is known, this is the only representation of a bed other than the sleigh type with such hangings. On sleigh beds, it might be mentioned that several modern students have stated that they were always placed parallel to the wall in the same fashion as this bed. Joseph Meeks' famous furniture advertisement, however, also shows a sleigh bed with its head against the wall and a narrower set of hangings, and European pictures also illustrate this method of placing such beds. Thus it is quite probable that sleigh beds could be arranged either way. Otherwise this Christmas scene indicates the stockings hung on the fireplace but no other seasonal decorations, in what is quite obviously an all-purpose room.

Plate 78. "Louisa's token of love to Mary," engraving from *Mary Grey; or, The Faithful Nurse*, Philadelphia, 1849. Courtesy Vera Craig.

This instructive and uplifting volume offers two scenes of the bedroom shared by Louisa and her nurse Mary Grey. One is a daytime scene; the other, shown here, is a night tableau. The most interesting difference is the presence in this picture of the whale oil lamp on the stand at the foot of the bed. This is the earliest picture yet found of a modern-type shade on such a lamp. None of these shades have actually survived so students still wonder about their construction. Probably they were paper on a wire frame just like their descendants, and so very perishable. Still, pictures such as this suggest that the bare lamps usually encountered in refurnished rooms today do not reflect the way the lamps actually appeared in use. The shades applied to modern electrifications of these lamps are actually much more accurate! Other points of interest are the drapes, described as chintz in the book, and the wall-to-wall carpeting.

Louisa's token of love to Mary.

Plate 79. *The Ernest Fiedler Family* by F. Heinrich, oil, 1850. Courtesy of the owner, Mrs. William L. Rich.

In the handsome drawing room at 38 Bond Street, Victorian opulence has been superimposed upon the classic revival architecture. A Renaissance-style painting of a Madonna faces the caryatids on the fireplace. The crystal and gilt chandelier is complemented by matching candelabra with decorated shades for the candles. The popular figured wall-to-wall carpeting is supplemented by a hearth rug of the same material, a practice that won acceptance even among the well-to-do who hoped to prolong the life of their floor covering by protecting it from the stray hot coals and extra wear that might be expected in that area. Finally, a fringed silk or satin cloth is thrown over the piano, foreshadowing the widespread use of such throw cloths in the second half of the century.

Plate 80. *The Hollingsworth Family* by George Hollingsworth, oil, c. 1850. Courtesy Museum of Fine Arts, Boston, M. & M. Karolik Collection.

George Hollingsworth recorded his large and distinguished family about 1850. At first glance the painting seems devoid of significant detail, but closer observation will ferret out a number of interesting bits. In the lower right corner, for instance, lie a burgonet, breastplate and gauntlet from a suit of black and white German armor of the late 16th century. They may be artistic props, family heirlooms or evidence of the growing interest in the Renaissance. Above the iron stove in the fireplace is a narrow painting, possibly done by Hollingsworth, to decorate a filler strip. Since it is summer the empty stove opening is filled with a vase and bouquet, but the hearth rug remains in place. A hard look at the window reveals that the drapes are either lined or that there are glass curtains behind them that have also been pulled aside by the tie-back. Then, of course, there is the family spaniel, attesting to the continued popularity of that breed.

Plate 81.   *A miner at Rough and Ready* (California) by Henry Walton, pen, ink and watercolor, 1853. Warren Howell Collection.

William D. Peck's cabin was strictly utilitarian as Henry Walton saw it. It was a dwelling such as a man might make himself when he had other more important things to do—like prospecting for gold. Even the home-made writing-arm chair had legs that did not match, but it held the important balance scale efficiently. Open shelves, pegs and chests or trunks provided the simplest forms of storage for those things which could not sit safely on the floor. There had been no time for frills or decoration, and the only color in the room is supplied by the blue and white patchwork quilt on Peck's bunk.

Plate 82.   *Saturday Night at the Mines* by Charles Nahl, oil, 1856. Stanford Museum Collections, Stanford University Museum.

Charles Nahl, who actually worked in the gold fields, recorded a more communal dwelling than Henry Walton had, but if one can peer through the shadows, he indicates a generally similar interior. The furniture is crude and probably made by the occupants. This time a table supports the gold scale, illuminated by a candle stuck in a bottle. Above the heads of the seated miners a companion sleeps in his bunk on the wall. Since Peck apparently lived alone, he had only one bunk. This one quite probably had a lower as well as an upper, and possibly more bunks outside the scope of the picture. The beams are exposed, and there seems to be only one layer of boards—just the siding, no sheathing. Even in California this must have afforded drafty quarters, making the fire, the blankets and the bottled spirits all welcome.

Plate 83. *The Luck of Roaring Camp* by Oscar
Kunath, oil, 1870–1875. By the permission of
the M. H. de Young Memorial Museum, San
Francisco.

Oscar Kunath undoubtedly painted his
genre scene after Bret Harte's story of the
same name appeared in 1870. Yet his illustration agrees with the earlier paintings by
Walton and Nahl. The dim interior with no
indication of an open window, the double
bunk, the home-made furniture, exposed
beams and dirt floor are much the same. In
the foreground clearly visible is a bench with
V-cut feet of the same form as that in the picture of Mrs. Sockbasin in 1817 (plate 27).

Plate 84. *The Sailor's Wedding* by Richard Caton Woodville, oil, 1852. Courtesy the Walters Art Gallery.

In the middle years of the last century a magistrate's office might well have been in his home. Here the elderly gentleman is interrupted at his lunch (which he is eating European fashion with the fork in his left hand) by a young couple intent on matrimony. His desk is a very fine Chippendale table which has had what appears to be a leather covering tacked over its top. The mirror is hung on the side of the cupboard next to the window for good light, and the wall decorations consist of a calendar and a map, both hung by tacks. There is a half curtain hung on a cord in typical cottage fashion. And, as might be anticipated in a room where the general public is expected, there is a cuspidor and a bare floor.

Plate 85. *The Windmill* by F. W. Edmonds, oil, 1850–1860. Courtesy the New-York Historical Society, New York City.

Edmonds' second kitchen picture of the 1850's portrays the same bare floor, exposed ceiling beams, and cupboard. It is distinguished, however, by a cooking stove built into the fireplace and by a water heater installed next to it. Stoves were just then beginning to make their appearance, but they did not catch on immediately. President Millard Fillmore (1850–1853) had been the first President to install a stove in the White House, but the cook refused to use it. "In the sixties and seventies," wrote Pauline Taft in *The Happy Valley,* "it was a mark of social standing not only to have a bathroom but also to have a cook stove in the kitchen." But even then, Mrs. Taft had to admit that when her family installed a cook stove at "Woodbine" their cook also refused to use it.

Plate 86. *Shake Hands* by Lily Martin Spencer, lithograph after the original painting published by W. Schaus, New York, 1854. Chicago Historical Society.

As a woman, Lily Martin Spencer knew well what a kitchen was like, and her humorous painting shows many interesting details aside from the floury hand being offered in greeting. The floor is covered with a patterned material, probably oilcloth. The cheery iron stove sits on a metal plate for fire safety. The older fireplace has been closed by a pictorial screen, and the mantel holds both a candlestick and a whale oil lamp along with the little ceramic lamb group which appears to have been very popular. The table with its turned legs was probably originally intended for more elegant purposes, and the ubiquitous backless chair which seems to have been present in almost every kitchen has been pressed into service to hold a pan of apples. It is at once a practical and a cheerful kitchen that bears little resemblance to its more antiseptic descendants.

Plate 87. *The Christmas Turkey* by F. W. Edmonds, oil, c. 1855. Courtesy the New-York Historical Society, New York City.

Edmonds' humorous confrontation between salesman and customer reinforces the evidence given by William Sidney Mount some twenty years earlier (Plate 48) concerning the lack of clutter on a working hearth. Here there are only a kettle and tongs. Like the earlier Mount drawing, the wall holds a board with nails or pegs for hanging a kerchief and a ring. The floor also is bare, and the walls either bare plaster or whitewashed. In keeping with the Woodville drawing (plate 75), the ledge on the cupboard holds miscellaneous utensils of recent use, while according to long custom the cat reflects absolute comfort and relaxation.

Plate 88. *Young Cook with Bird* by Enoch Wood Perry, Jr., pencil and wash, 1859. Courtesy the Walters Art Gallery.

In this group of mid 19th century kitchens the pictures have shown both bare wood and oilcloth-covered floors. This drawing depicts a brick floor with a throw rug in front of the table for ease in standing and possibly warmth on a cold day. Here, too, there is a cook stove, and a bouquet in a tumbler standing before the shelf clock. It might be noted also that this is the youngest and best-dressed cook of the lot!

Plate 89. *Girl and Pets* by Eastman Johnson, oil, 1856. In the collection of The Corcoran Gallery of Art.

Calm and sweetness pervade Eastman Johnson's canvas in this almost cloyingly Victorian composition, yet the artist manages to include a wealth of detail about the paraphernalia of household pets of the time as well as one or two other interesting sidelights on American homes. The goldfish bowl has the same globe and pedestal form as one depicted by Samuel F. B. Morse about twenty years earlier in *The Goldfish Bowl,* a painting that was not available for this study. Thus far these are the only two known paintings that show one of these bowls. The cage for the guinea pigs, however, is a unique record, illustrated nowhere else. The bars on the side appear wooden, but this seems hardly likely in a cage for a rodent. They must have been metal, and the tops and bottoms must also have had wire or sheet metal linings to prevent the animals from gnawing their way out. The parrot sits on a simple wooden T-cross perch on a flat base. It is held fast by a chain from one leg to the upright. Only the cat has complete freedom. Another very interesting detail is the euphorbia growing in the large pot against the wall. This is the earliest known picture of a euphorbia cultivated as a decorative plant in an American home. The room itself seems to be a storage chamber of some sort, but this is entirely secondary to the living things that inhabit it.

Plate 90. *The Image Pedlar* by Francis W. Edmonds, oil, 1850–1858. Courtesy the New-York Historical Society, New York City.

In this more ambitious composition than the preceding two, Edmonds betrays a striving for the quaint. Still, some of the details are valid. The half curtain on a string is quite typical of a simple dwelling. So is the dry sink with the bench next to it in the kitchen visible through the door at the right. The several shelves on brackets, the musket, wag-on-the-wall clock, print tacked on the wall, clothes hanging on pegs, and bare floor are all features that one would expect. An unusual feature, on the other hand, is the bottle hung by a cord around its neck in the window opening. Its purpose is a mystery.

Plate 91. *Mrs. A. W. Smith's Parlor, Broad & Spruce Streets* by Joseph Shoemaker Russell, watercolor, 1853. Collection of Bertram K. and Nina Fletcher Little.

There has seldom been a more literal recorder of room interiors than Joseph Russell. Here he shows the formal room of what was quite probably a boarding house in Philadelphia. The windows are completely drapeless in this summer scene, but the walls are papered to about 18 inches below the ceiling. The floor is covered with wall-to-wall carpeting. The mantel bears a formal arrangement with a bouquet in the center, two urns and two figurines, but there are no pictures on the walls. Most interesting, perhaps, is the table on cast iron supports of the type which later came to be associated with sewing machines. It supports the gas lamp with its rigid pipe coming out from the wall and making two right-angle turns. Another fascinating detail is the loose covering on the back of the armchair in the left foreground. It is an early appearance of an enlarged version of the later Victorian and Edwardian antimacassar.

Plate 92.   *Dining Room at Mrs. Smith's* by Joseph S. Russell, watercolor, 1853. Collection of Bertram K. and Nina Fletcher Little.

Mrs. Smith's dining room was apparently just as devoid of ornament as her parlor. The only thing that could possibly be considered decorative is the placement of two tiny whale oil lamps on the mantel. Even then, one wonders if these could actually have been for light rather than ornament. There is no other lighting fixture visible. An outlet for gas appears on the wall above the serving table, but no pipe or lamp has been attached to it. The windows, interestingly enough, have both shutters and roller shades with short tassels for pulls. This seems very early for spring-loaded rollers, but Mr. Russell, perhaps through oversight, does not indicate any cords or pulleys. Studying the table setting involves a bit of guesswork at this scale, but it does appear that there are no spoons, just knives and forks at each place, and that each setting has its own individual salt shaker. The floor may be bare or covered with canvas or straw matting. It is not carpeted, which is what one might have expected. As frugal a boarding house keeper as Mrs. Smith seems to have been, she would not have wanted to subject an expensive carpet to the dining vagaries of assorted guests.

Plate 93. *Mr. J. S. Russell's Room at Mrs. Smith's* . . . by Joseph S. Russell, water-color, 1853. Collection of Bertram K. and Nina Fletcher Little.

Like the rest of Mrs. Smith's house, the walls of Joseph Russell's room are papered, but the touches of decoration suggest that perhaps they were added by the boarder himself. The silhouettes and miniatures on the chimney breast, the fine vases and the candlesticks on the mantel seem unlikely pieces for a rented room unless the resident was a very special boarder indeed. Other nice touches are the coverlet on the bed and the runners on the two chests of drawers. As a transient, Mr. Russell has placed his trunk in one corner and has boxes on the shelf with tied paper covers. Curtains hanging from the shelf cover additional storage space. In this room the floor seems quite definitely to be covered with straw matting.

Plate 94. *Misses Russell's room at Mrs. A. W. Smith . . .* by Joseph S. Russell, watercolor, 1853. Collection of Bertram K. and Nina Fletcher Little.

In this and the following picture, Mr. Russell illustrates his daughters' room as it appeared in two different years as these young ladies practiced the ever popular feminine pastime of rearranging furniture. Every piece of furniture is the same in both scenes; it has merely been shifted around. The one major alteration is the disappearance of the large box-like structure protruding from the right wall in the earlier watercolor. Probably this provided storage for clothes and other personal belongings so the girls must have found another location for it—or persuaded their father to let them keep their surplus things in his storage area. Otherwise this room is a little nicer than Mr. Russell's room in that it has a carpeted floor. Like the other rooms (except the dining room) it also has folding shutters on the inside of the windows in addition to the louvered shutters on the outside.

Plate 95. *Sarah & Eliza Russell's room at Mrs. Smith's* . . . by Joseph S. Russell, watercolor, 1854. Collection of Bertram K. and Nina Fletcher Little.

Along with the furniture changes in the Russell girls' room, one can note that they have removed the antimacassar from the cylindrical pillow of the day bed and cleared the mantel except for a small vase with a bouquet. With the little table moved to the center of the room, Mr. Russell has given a clearer picture of the whale oil lamp with its very modern-looking shade.

Plate 96. *A Domestic Tragedy* by an unknown artist, oil, 1850–1860. Collection of Mr. & Mrs. Samuel Schwartz.

This traumatic scene of the broken pitcher and clock was purchased in New Jersey and quite probably represents a farmhouse in that area. Even at this late date the floor is bare in this modest dwelling, and there are neither drapes nor curtains though there does appear to be a shade. The pictures are hung over ornamental nails on exceptionally long cords, but perhaps the real center of interest from a decorative standpoint is the red painted rocker. It boasts separate green cushions on both the seat and back, and there is a white antimacassar with rose embroidery pinned at the top. To complete the color scheme the walls are a putty color, and the sofa is upholstered in green. The chairs, of course, are black with yellow bands.

Plate 97. *The Picture Book* by John George Brown, pencil, 1859. Courtesy The Walters Art Gallery.

Sentimental and syrupy though it may be, this archetypal Victorian drawing still indicates the use of a fitted slipcover on a sofa that covers the wood of the legs without the use of a skirt. It is enough to make it a useful document.

Plate 98. *George T. Trimble* by Thomas Hicks, oil, 1854. Courtesy Museum of the City of New York.

George T. Trimble was superintendent of schools in New York City and the doorway in which he stands is quite probably that of a school rather than his home. Nevertheless it offers the opportunity to introduce a subject of much importance to modern domestic interiors—the wastepaper basket. The earliest representation of one of these homely containers appears in a portrait of Hamilton Fish in his office painted two years earlier, in 1852, but it is not so clear a picture as this one. Generally speaking, wastepaper baskets were not an object of domestic necessity in those days. They appear about mid century in school rooms, politicians' offices and the studies of authors. As late as 1900 there was so little demand for wastepaper baskets that Sears Roebuck & Company did not even include them in their great compilations of the physical needs and desires of Americans. There was not the overpowering flood of paper that inundates the homes of today. Such excess as there was was either salvaged or fed into the open fires. The baskets that were used were almost always wickerwork like the one shown here. Exceptions include the use of a laundry basket by Robert E. Lee (plate 135) and of the family leather firebucket by Dr. John H. Brinton as shown in Thomas Eakin's portrait of him in 1876 (National Gallery of Art, Washington).

Plate 99. *James Fenimore Cooper's Library* by an unknown artist, pencil, c. 1850–1860. Courtesy of the New York State Historical Association, Cooperstown.

This sketch, which has come down through the Cooper family, has traditionally been identified as the great novelist's library in Otsego Hall. There is no doubt about its location, but if it was drawn during James Fenimore's lifetime, it is one of the earliest representations of the use of the Moorish arch in American interior decoration. Cooper died in 1851. Everything else seems quite in keeping with the period—the covered writing table with the wicker wastepaper basket beneath it, the tiny vases with their little bouquets on the mantel, the hearth rug, and all the rest. In this summer scene the fireplace is left open and vacant with no attempt at disguise. Perhaps the rest of the room is so busy with patterns that the owners felt the fireplace could be ignored.

Plate 100. *Washington Irving's Library, Sunnyside, March 16, 1860* by Daniel Huntington, pencil. Courtesy the Cooper-Hewitt Museum of Design, Smithsonian Institution.

A good friend of Irving's, Daniel Huntington visited his home, Sunnyside, a few months after the writer's death and made three sketches of his library on the ground floor. This sketch shows the north end of the room from behind the double pedestal "partner's" desk. The wicker wastepaper basket stands at the left and at the right is Irving's chair in the late classical style. This chair, which was a favorite of the writer, is the subject of a separate sketch, also in the Cooper-Hewitt Museum. The bookcases are built in, and the wall paneling is bird's eye maple. The curtains carry a note stating they are "thin white." Benson J. Lossing, who visited Sunnyside at about the same time, sketched the same room from the opposite side, showing the front of the desk, and he notes that the curtains are lace. Lossing also shows the bookcase-lined sleeping alcove with its divan and separate cushions curtained off with "plain Turkey red curtains" tied back by ribbons. This drawing is in the Lossing Collection of the Henry E. Huntington Library and Art Gallery.

Plate 101. *Library Sunnyside—March 16/60* by Daniel Huntington, pencil, 1860. Courtesy the Cooper-Hewitt Museum of Design, Smithsonian Institution.

The second of Daniel Huntington's sketches of Washington Irving's library shows the northeast corner with its marble fireplace, coal grate and mantel arrangement of two two-branched bronze candelabra and two watercolors in maple frames with gilt edges. Above the fireplace is an engraving in a gilt frame, and Irving's gray slouch hat and dark coat hang on a hook on the back of the door. Between the door and fireplace is a low bookcase. With the three Huntington sketches and the Lossing sketch still extant, this celebrated library is one of the best documented rooms of the period. It has been recreated by Sleepy Hollow Restorations as part of an exceptionally successful historical restoration.

Plate 102. "Backgrounds of Civilization—Establishment of Mr. Glennan and His Full-headed Family," woodcut from *New York Illustrated News,* February 11, 1860. Courtesy New York State Library.

Pictures of slum dwellings are excessively rare, and those that do exist are often weak in credibility because they were drawn for propaganda purposes. The illustrations in such highly moral contemporary stories as *Hot Corn* are a case in point. This plate and the next illustrate two of the best pictures of hovels that have thus far been discovered. They were done as part of a crusading article, it is true, and unsympathetic as well, but they do purport to portray actual dwellings in the Dutch Hill section of New York City, and they have a validity of appearance that the book illustrations normally lack. In this era it was most often Irish immigrant families who lived in the big city slums as they awaited the opportunity to move up the social and economic scale. The crucifixion picture on the wall, and the name of the family strongly suggest the family shown here are representatives of this group. And there is also a strong suggestion that they are slothful and lazy and largely responsible for their own unhappy situation.

Plate 103. "Backgrounds of Civilization—Interior of Mr. John Bradley's Cottage. His Family and Fellow-lodgers," woodcut from the *New York Illustrated News,* February 11, 1860. Courtesy New York State Library.

Again the artist has strongly suggested the Irish origin of this slum family and its Roman Catholicism through the religious pictures on the walls, the facial characteristics of the family, and the pigs in the living room. In so doing he undoubtedly struck a number of responsive chords among the prejudices of his better-established viewers.

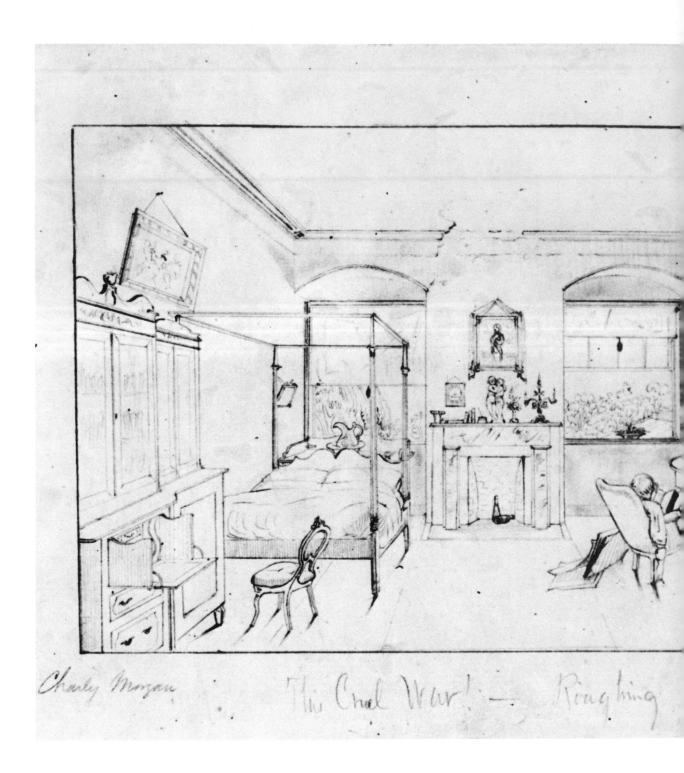

Charley Morgan · The Civil War! — Roughing

at (Arlington 14

Plate 104. *The Civil War—Roughing it at Arlington House* by Charly Morgan, pencil, 1862. Courtesy Custis-Lee Mansion, National Park Service.

When Robert E. Lee's family moved out of Arlington House, some of the Union soldiers guarding Washington had the good luck to bivouac in the mansion. Charly Morgan was one of these, and his meticulously accurate drawing shows one of the bedrooms during his occupancy. Actually it remained almost exactly as the Lee family had left it. Charly's only additions seem to be the bottles in the fireplace, the saber and kepi on the wall and perhaps some of the books and boxes. There is, of course, the question of how many things the Lees took away with them. Ornaments such as the statuette of The Three Graces on the mantel (which is mentioned specifically in contemporary documents) stayed behind, but there may have been bed hangings (though this is a summer scene) and perhaps window draperies or curtains. The windows still have roller shades with tassel pulls, and the floor appears to have a covering of strips of straw matting or possibly canvas. Especially interesting is the portrait over the fireplace with a scarf or sash draped over it. This could be a personal memento or it might signify mourning if it is black. The pictures are hung on exposed cords or wires over ornamental pins, and they are decidedly angled out from the wall. The location of the washstand in front of the window at the head of the bed may seem an odd location until one realizes that it does place the mirror next to the window for light, and this seems to have been a prime consideration in furniture arrangement until the introduction of the electric light.

Plate 105. *Winter Quarters in Virginia—Army of the Potomac, 1864* by George Cochran Lambdin, oil, 1866. Courtesy Berry-Hill Galleries, N. Y.

George Cochran Lambdin painted a number of pictures related to the Civil War, the best known of which are perhaps this scene and *The Consecration*. The sources of his information, however, are unknown. He may have visited the encampments before Petersburg where this scene is located in person— or he may have had descriptions or sketches from veterans. In any event, the features he shows accord well with written descriptions. The log walls offer more warmth than the canvas alone, and a stick and mud chimney will serve as long as there is plenty of mud between the fire and the sticks. Here a wooden box serves as a cupboard, and there are a hand-made table and bench in addition to the store-bought folding camp chair. Presumably there is a folding cot behind the viewer, also sitting on the floor of packed Virginia clay.

Plate 106. "Inside View of a Log Hut," woodcut by Charles W. Reed from *Hard Tack and Coffee* by John D. Billings, 1888.

The huts used by enlisted men for semi-permanent winter quarters during the Civil War did not differ materially from those of officers. More men lived in less space, and they had fewer store-bought comforts, but the log walls, dirt floor and canvas roof were the same. Here the men have double bunks built across the end wall, and probably another set fastened to the opposite end out of view. They have fashioned a bench and stool from split logs and constructed a table from a wooden box. Their arms and equipment hang on wall pegs just like those of the officers, and the mantel shelf holds a candle, cups and plates. The fireplace, here recessed, is probably built of mud sticks though sometimes soldiers "found" bricks and mortar. Chimneys might also be stick or even a barrel with the heads knocked out. Both the artist and the author of the book he illustrated served in the Army of the Potomac during the war so they were thoroughly familiar with interiors of this sort.

Plate 107. *My Cabin, Elk Creek, Montana Territory* by Peter P. Tofft, oil, 1866.
Courtesy Museum of Fine Arts, Boston, M. and M. Karolik Collection.

Tofft's simple western cabin was in many ways similar to the huts of the soldiers at Petersburg. He did have a wooden roof and a glazed window, however,
even two roughly framed pictures. Otherwise there is the same combination of
commercial folding chair and locally made table, all sitting on the typical dirt
floor. The principal difference lies in the fact that the food containers and other
gear are civilian rather than military. Among these, locally made containers of
wood and leather predominate over the few metal cooking utensils. There is the
same sort of food or coffee grinder attached to the wall that Walton illustrated in
William Peck's California cabin in 1853 (plate 81). The bag suspended from the
ceiling quite probably holds flour or some other foodstuff that needed to be kept
dry.

Plate 108. *Slaves Concealing their Master from a Search Party* from *Confederate War Etchings* by Adalbert J. Volck, 1862. Library of Congress.

As a Southern sympathizer, Volck naturally portrayed the living conditions of the slaves and their relationship to their master in the best possible light. Here the faithful servants are shown in a simple but comfortable room, very similar to those lived in by working class whites and farmers (See plate 111). The brick hearth of the cooking fireplace is completely free from clutter as it would have been in any working kitchen. This was an all-purpose room for living, cooking, eating and sleeping. The bed may be seen at the right with clothing hanging from nails or pegs on the wall behind the slave owner. The walls would appear to be plastered, and the window shade which rolls up like a porch blind is an interesting detail.

Plate 109.   *Fireplace in a Negro shanty, near Culpeper Court House, Va., April 25, 1864*
by Edwin Forbes, pencil. Library of Congress.

Edwin Forbes found that all slave cabins were not as comfortable as the one
depicted by Adalbert Volck. Perhaps this one had been largely abandoned except for the andirons, the tin pot and the axe, but even so the fireplace is a far cry
from the well-made example in the previous plate and the walls are rough log instead of plastered. There are few details, but this vignette suggests a much more
primitive setting for living.

Plate 110. *The Warning* by Edward Lamson Henry, oil, 1865. Courtesy Hirschl and Adler Galleries, Inc., New York City.

In this spirited scene three soldiers of the 104th Pennsylvania Volunteers are warned of approaching enemy by a Negro youth in whose home they had been resting and enjoying refreshments. This may have been a slave cabin or the home of free Negroes, though the latter seems more likely. The furniture is simple. The walls are bare wood, unplastered. The floor is bare except for the small rug before the cookstove. This stove is a surprising item since cookstoves were not yet universal in the North. This one sits on bricks to insulate it from the wooden floor, and a supply of firewood is piled beneath it. The window at the left has a half curtain hung on a string, and there is a skirt on the bracket shelf next to it. Utensils are placed by the stove or hung from pegs on the wall above it in a very convincing manner except for the mirror which would have been virtually useless in the dark corner. All in all, it seems a reasonably believable compromise between the sterile quality of the Volck and the primitive discomfort of the Forbes, though there may well have been actual counterparts of all three.

Plate 111. "Interior of Bennett Place," from *Harper's Weekly*, May 27, 1865, woodcut. Courtesy State Department of Archives and History, Raleigh, N. C.

Gen. Joseph E. Johnston surrendered the last major Confederate army in the field to Gen. William T. Sherman in this simple North Carolina home, Bennett Place. It has been restored and is now operated as a state historic site. The walls and floor are bare wood, and the ceiling is unfinished. The only attempt at decoration is a drape nailed to the window molding, and pulled to one side where it is again tacked. A mirror and a spring scale hang side by side on the stair wall. It is, in fact, not radically different from the Negro home in plate 108. The only thing that does set it apart is the quality of the furnishings. The chair and clock are only average, but the candlestand and drop-leaf table look quite good, and so does the crib, a corner of which can be seen at the far right. Such contradictions were not uncommon in rural American homes of the period and area. In nearby Tennessee, Charles C. Nott of the 5th Iowa Cavalry commented on the contrasts: ". . . in half the houses you will find pianos, and half the women play by note. In this house the ceiling is not plastered; the unpainted mantel is covered with broken bottles and old candlesticks; the rough log walls are adorned with two-penny engravings cut from almanacs and country papers; all the furniture in the house is not worth $5. But there is a piano, a handsome one, with a showy cover." It is quite likely that the owners of these homes saw nothing unusual in the contrasts. To them consistency would have had no virtue whatsoever. They used the best things they could acquire as soon as they could acquire them and hoped that eventually everything would be brought to that level.

Plate 112. *Lunch Time* by Eastman Johnson, oil, 1865. Courtesy Colby College Art Museum.

The humbler homes in the North during the middle 19th century tended to be a bit larger than those in the rural South. Probably this is because many of them were older houses that had become unfashionable or that stood in neighborhoods no longer considered desirable. Halls are perhaps the least illustrated part of a house, but in this painting Eastman Johnson shows one from a poor family's home. The door is weathered and unpainted, and the plaster on the wall has fallen off in large areas. The floor is bare in both the hall and the bedroom that is visible through the door, but there is a hooked or yarn-sewn rug before the door and another small rug of indeterminate type beside the low post bed. The bedclothes hang down to the floor and seem to cover the pillows. Corncobs, the almost universal plaything of farm children, lie on the floor. Here they have been used as logs to build a fort and, with a pair of wheels, to form a cannon.

Plate 113. *Caught in the Act* by Tompkins H. Matteson, oil, c. 1860–1864. Collection of the Vassar College Art Gallery, gift of Matthew Vassar 1864.

Few other pictures offer the wealth of detail of kitchen and scullery furnishings that T. H. Matteson has brought to his portrayal of a young culprit who has inadvertently broken a pot of coffee or spices in his quest for something tempting in the little cupboard. Here are excellent depictions of the method of covering jars with paper or cloth and string that has been shown in other pictures but not so clearly. The Windsor chair minus its back that seems to have found ubiquitous use in kitchens had served as his perch, and there is an extra heavy table, almost a butcher's block, holding the duck and vegetables for dinner. In the kitchen proper a young lady irons flatwork on a cloth thrown over a table with an open pot for sprinkling, and a laundry basket handy on the floor at her side. The window has full curtains hung on a string, and there is a covering on the floor though the backroom has only unpainted boards. It is, in all, a scene that conveys every evidence of a practical and living milieu.

Plate 114.   *Corn Shelling* by Eastman Johnson, oil, 1864. The Toledo Museum of Art, Toledo, Ohio; gift of Florence Scott Libbey, 1924.

In this fine genre scene Eastman Johnson shows a simple farm kitchen that has been equipped with one of the new iron cookstoves. The old fireplace has been partially bricked up behind it for a connection though the stove pipe goes up in front of it before presumably connecting with the old chimney. Now two flatirons sit on the brick while a colander, tin lantern and basket hang on the chimney breast above. An iron teakettle and a tin pot sit on the stove top. There is a general absence of paint, and the floor is bare. The old man shells the corn into a box, using a board sheller cut with a handhold, in the light from the open door. Here Johnson has been especially successful in suggesting the level of illumination in a day when artificial light was used only at night. Few modern families would tolerate the light level that was the norm before the 20th century.

Plate 115. *Whittling a Boat* by Henry Bacon, oil, 1867. Courtesy Kennedy Galleries, Inc., New York City.

In another mid-century New England kitchen scene, Henry Bacon confirms the evidence of other artists and adds details of pot and pan storage plus a dry sink beneath the window. The floor is somewhat a puzzle. The boards of the trap-door at the left are clearly shown, but none are shown on the floor proper. This may have been intended to indicate a floor covering of some sort or it may be artistic license, intended to de-emphasize that area.

Plate 116.   "Making Sausage in the Old Manner" by Henry Barott, woodcut from *'S Alt Marik-Haus in D'r Schtadt un Die Alte Zeite' Ein Centennial Poem in Pennsylfanish Dutsch* by H. L. Fischer, York, Pennsylvania, 1879. From the Collection of the Historical Society of York County in York, Pa.

In this picture of sausage-making in Pennsylvania about mid century, Henry Barott illustrates many of the ways in which kitchens in the Pennsylvania Dutch tradition differed from their counterparts in both the North and the South. Also he offers a night scene with the light provided by a candle held in the so-called chamberstick and a Betty lamp hung on the shelf in addition to the fire. The fireplace itself is a point of departure. There is no cookstove here, and the fire is built on the hearth without andirons, in one of the latest representations of this Pennsylvania Dutch technique. Again there is a heavy table or butcher's block on which the boys cut up the meat. The technique in which the head of the family presses the handle of the sausage stuffer against his chest is an interesting detail, as is the use of a string between nails on the wall and mantel for holding ladles.

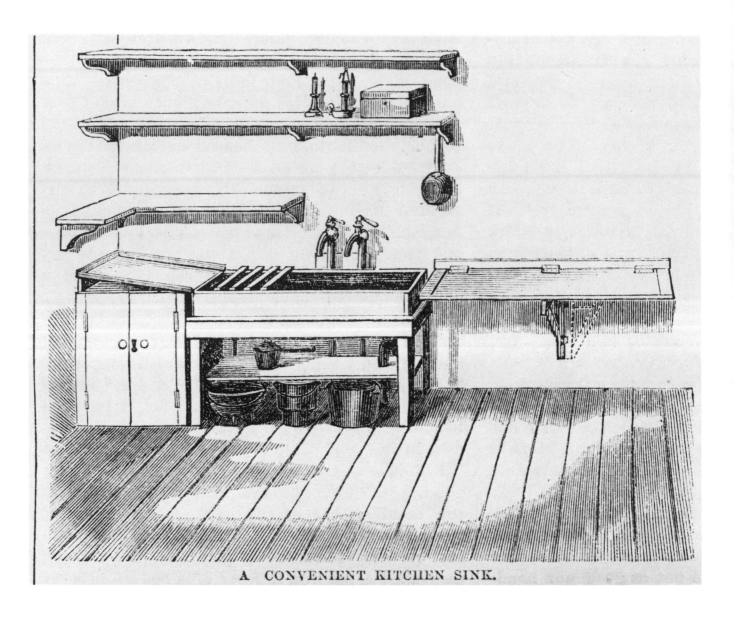

A CONVENIENT KITCHEN SINK.

Plate 117. "A Convenient Kitchen Sink," woodcut from *The American Agriculturist,* February 1865. Courtesy Vera Craig.

The American Agriculturist took great pains to advise its rural readers of the best manner for designing, doing or arranging for every conceivable activity (almost). Here they recommend a sink design for those farm families able to avail themselves of running water. There are faucets for hot and cold water, shelves for dishes, candlesticks and other utensils, and a slanted drainboard as well as a folding table and a cupboard. Lucky indeed would be the farm family who could have this modern a kitchen. Running water was still primarily a city luxury in 1865—and a big eastern city at that. Many rural homes still had dry sinks, or at best an inside pump, well into the present century.

Plate 118. "A Method of Arranging a Kitchen," woodcut from *The American Agriculturist*, April 1876. Courtesy Vera Craig.

Eleven years after the sink shown in the previous plate, *The American Agriculturist* offered a design that would be much more practical for the average American farm family. Here there is a pump for the sink rather than hot and cold running water. Otherwise it is a much more sophisticated kitchen with closed cupboards, some with glass doors, a wire drainboard, even a pantry with a pass-through. As in all other kitchen pictures of the 19th century, the floor is bare. The only covering ever shown is an occasional oilcloth. The rugs seen in some modern refurnishings are completely out of period. Since this does represent the 1870's, there is a vase of greenery and a pot with a growing plant on the shelf by the pantry door. Americans of that era wanted greenery in every possible room.

A METHOD OF ARRANGING A KITCHEN.

Plate 119. *Entrance hall of Mr. Charles Green's House in Savannah, Ga., now occupied by Gen. Sherman as headquarters* by William Waud, pencil and wash, December 1864. Library of Congress.

Quite a contrast to the simpler cabins of soldiers and prospectors and the plain New England kitchens is the hall of the Green house, a palatial residence that still stands. Its marble floor, beamed ceiling and ornate moldings bespeak the finest in a town house of Savannah. There are gas chandeliers and wall lights while the collection of classical and religious statuary and pictures give the home the air of a museum or public building. Of most interest from the standpoint of documenting ephemera are the huge plants in their wooden pots set on cross bases. The presence of the handles on these pots suggest that they were probably kept outside in the warmer months and then brought indoors during the winter.

Plate 120. *Bedroom of William Clark, East End* by Alfred R. Waud, pencil, 1865. Library of Congress.

Almost everyone is familiar with the west end of William Clark's bedroom. This was the room in which Abraham Lincoln died in a walnut spool bed "too short for his frame." Dozens of engravings and paintings show this scene, sometimes stretching the small room to gigantic proportions in order to accommodate all the prominent figures gathered about the bed. Few artists, however, bothered to record the other end of the room. Waud was the exception. Right after the tragic event he visited the room with his sketchbook and made rapid notes of its appearance. These were just reminders for a future newspaper illustration, and actually he never used them. Still they offer considerable information about a bedroom of the era.

William Clark was a young Massachusetts soldier assigned to the Quartermaster Department in Washington, and he rented this first floor bedroom in the home of William Petersen, a tailor. Probably most of the furnishings belonged to Petersen, including the considerable number of horse pictures. The large picture at the right is an engraving of J. H. Herring's "Village Blacksmith." Others included "The Stable," "Barnyard" and, not shown, a photograph of "The Horse Fair" by Rosa Bonheur. A Sheraton style commode or washstand sits beneath the blacksmith engraving where it would have been just at the foot of the bed. Clark's trunk rests in the corner, and his clothes hang from a rack on the wall beneath a disconnected stovepipe. On the left wall there is a gas lamp with an interesting shade above a drop-leaf table, and in the lower left corner a portion of the dresser and mirror can be seen. The two windows have roller shades with tassel pulls but no drapes or curtains. On the ceiling Waud noted that the room had "drab paper" and sketched the designs. Actually the wallpaper was a brownish color with white figures, and the floor was covered by a "worn Brussells carpet." Lodgers, it seems, have seldom lived in stylish rooms.

Plate 121. *Bedroom, Joseph Henry's Quarters, Smithsonian Institution,* photograph, 1860–1870. Courtesy the Smithsonian Institution.

In the early days of the Smithsonian, the Secretary was granted living space in the building on the Mall. The exact date of this photograph of one of the bedrooms is unknown, but it must have been made during the 1860's. The problem of treating large arched windows has been skillfully handled with dark drapes and lace glass curtains. The bed has a fringed coverlet that hangs over the sideboards, and the spool table at the foot has a matching fringed runner beneath the small bowl of flowers and the books. The marble-topped dresser, on the other hand, is bare except for the bottles and other toiletries which stand upon it. The furniture is an interesting mixture with two late klismos type side chairs of the early part of the century and a folding chair with a caned back blending with the Victorian pieces. The presence of a sofa in a bedroom is doubly interesting since there is one in the following photograph of a bedroom also. Ordinarily one would not consider it a piece of bedroom furniture. There is wall-to-wall carpeting, and for some reason the gas chandelier has no globes.

Plate 122. *Bedroom in which Joseph Henry Died,* photograph, 1860–1870. Courtesy Smithsonian Institution.

Joseph Henry did not die until 1878 and he seems to have been very much alive when this photograph was taken. Just look at the array of liquor bottles, glass, bowl with ladle and large bowl of flowers on the spool table at the foot of the bed as well as the garment thrown over the foot and the quilted dressing gown on the bed itself. Here again, the white coverlet hangs over the sideboards. This time one can see the pillow sham with lace edging at the head. The window treatment is the same as in the previous photograph though the materials are different. There is the same mixture of old and new furniture, but this time the marble-topped dresser seems to have a runner as well as the table. Note also the striped cover with fringe thrown over the caned back of the rocker near the window. It reflects but does not repeat the striping of the drapes and the sofa upholstery. The gas chandelier has its globes, and this time one can see an adjustable light at the head of the bed in one of the earliest bits of evidence for a reading light.

Plate 123. *Joseph Henry's Library*, photograph, 1860–1870. Courtesy Smithsonian Institution.

There are three chairs in this picture of a small corner of Joseph Henry's library, and all three are different. At the desk there is a wicker rocker. Facing it is a Gothic side chair, and just intruding into the lower left corner is a folding chair with a caned seat. Glass-fronted bookcases line the walls, and just at the very left one can see part of the frame of a picture hung directly on the front of one of the case doors. On the desk is a gas lamp, its frosted glass globe almost invisible against the white of the walls and bookcase framing. It is fed by a flexible rubber hose from the chandelier above.

Plate 124. *A Window, House on Hudson River* by Worthington Whittredge, oil, 1863. Courtesy New-York Historical Society, New York City.

Worthington Whittredge's rendering of this narrow high-ceilinged Victorian room illustrates many of the customs of the period. Since it is summer the carpet has been removed, leaving the floor bare except for the single Oriental rug. The drapes have been removed from the window and replaced by light curtains that follow the shape of the cornice at the top and are pulled back by ribbons and tie-backs. The curtains in this picture seem to be lace, but gauze and thin muslin might also be used. The purpose was to soften the direct sunlight and when dropped straight, to keep out insects. Heavy drapes and curtains, the Victorians thought, looked too warm for summertime. The paintings are hung well above eye level on long wires that run all the way up to a rod placed just a few inches below the ceiling. The window seat has a separate cushion apparently made in three pieces, and the facing below the seat bears stenciled decorations, a feature that has seldom been recorded.

Plate 125. *Trimming the Christmas Tree* by Lewis Lang, oil, 1865. Courtesy Kennedy Galleries, Inc., New York City.

A lonely German visitor in Williamsburg probably erected the first Christmas tree in America in the 1740's, but that was undoubtedly a lone exception. It was a century later before other German immigrants introduced the festive evergreen on a permanent basis—or so most authorities believe today. Here the tree is set on the floor in a bucket of sand or dirt. Other pictures of the same era show smaller trees in buckets placed on tables. Already shown here are glass ornaments and perhaps some gingerbread or cookie figures and there were also candleholders, tinsel and paper ornaments that appear in other pictures. Dimly seen in the background are festoons of evergreen ropes over the windows as additional Yuletide decorations.

Plate 126. *Visiting Grandma* by J. A. S. Oertel, oil, 1865. Courtesy Kennedy Galleries, Inc., New York City.

According to this painting Grandma was well advanced in years but very up to date in interior decoration. The furniture is in the latest style. The Rogers group of "The Town Pump" on the wall bracket had only been patented in 1862, and the gas lamp on the center table is very modern indeed. It is fed by a rubber hose from the chandelier above, and, indeed, even at the beginning of this century it was a standard witticism for older men, especially tall ones, to assure children that the primary purpose of the center table was to prevent grownups from banging their heads on the chandeliers. In this scene there are no less than three of these gas chandeliers—but only one center table!

Plate 127. *Sunday Morning, Rhode Island* by Eastman Johnson and Worthington Whittredge, oil, late 1860's. Courtesy Newhouse Galleries, Inc., New York City.

Good personal friends, Johnson and Whittredge here collaborated on a picture of a home in one of their favorite summer areas. Whittredge did the room itself, Johnson the figures. A spare, stark room, it may well strike viewers as being unrealistically bare, but it should be pointed out that both these artists were normally meticulous portrayers of domestic scenes. Johnson's pictures of homes in the New York City area are often very cluttered while all those that he painted during his regular visits to Rhode Island are simple and bare. Quite probably this is the way they actually were. Here the very fine Windsor chair contrasts with the simple slat back and the plain drop-leaf table, and the floor and walls are absolutely bare except for the clock on the shelf between the windows. The only decoration seems to be a vine growing in the hanging pot near the far window plus a few dried herbs. Another interesting detail, shown in no other pictures, is the musket hanging between the joists on the ceiling, near the center of the room. It would have been a good dry area, but difficult to reach—and this may actually have been the reason for the location if grandchildren were frequent visitors.

Plate 128. *Nantucket Interior* by Eastman Johnson, oil, 1865. Courtesy Kennedy Galleries, Inc., New York City.

In contrast to the very full and busy Victorian interiors shown in most pictures is this spare New England room dominated by the seated man with his clay pipe. The low ladderback chair with a separate cushion on its seat is an unusual type while the ginger jar on the improvised shelf by the mantel is a relic of an earlier era. It is interesting to note also that the fire on the hearth is built without andirons in the fashion usually associated with the Pennsylvania Dutch.

Plate 129. *Home Again,* lithograph by Endicott & Co., 1866. The Library of Congress.

In this sentimental scene depicting the return of a Union Army captain from the Civil War, the artist manages to include a number of interesting details of interior decoration and practice. The wall map that hung in so many homes of the 1860's and 1870's is very apparent here as is the interest in the sea evidenced by the seashell on the mantel and the large starfish on top of the mirror at the extreme right. The cup of spills for lighting the fire is a convincing detail next to the clock, and fans, of course, were also popular residents of mantels at that time. As a final wall note, the musket above the map is upside down, a position that a study of these contemporary pictures suggests may have been the case more often than not. The carpet, which consists of many narrow strips in a tartan check pattern, is a type that was probably quite popular because of its low cost, though it is seldom shown. The heavy lines dividing the strips suggest that they were overlapped rather than being sewed edge to edge, but this may be a misinterpretation. Next to the rocking chair at the right is a wicker basket of the type that was normally sold as a wastepaper basket in the 1860's. This is the only picture of such a basket in an ordinary home that has been found thus far, but even here it seems to have been used as a sewing basket and not for wastepaper.

THE FOUR SEASONS OF LIFE: M

The Season of Strength.

But as the hues of summer fade away,
And verging fast, to days of sober brown,
So Year advances, mingle with its hue,
And casts like age so rich pleasure's sting.

NEW YORK PUBLISHED BY CURRIER & IVES 152 NASSAU STREET

Plate 130. *The Four Seasons of Life: Middle Age,* lithograph by Currier & Ives, 1868. The Library of Congress.

The credibility quotient of Currier & Ives scenes of domestic interiors is unusually low, but this plate and the following print based on original pictures by J. M. Ives are quite good. This one also has the advantage of illustrating a hall and stairway. These stairs are carpeted with a runner held in place by rods in the same manner as the one shown many years earlier in plate 66. At the foot there is a shaggy throw rug which seems to serve no useful purpose unless it might be to cushion the bump of someone falling downstairs or the landing of a youngster sliding down the banister and over the newel post. In the narrow hall that presumably leads back to the kitchen is a typical hall rack for hats and coats with a mirror to assist in the proper positioning of the former. There is also a framed engraving suggesting that the attitude towards hallways was changing and that they were no longer to be ignored as mere passageways between more important areas. In the doorway is a pot of plants with a vine growing upwards that presages the profusion of vines and other greenery that came to dominate the interiors of the next decade. The dog is a retriever, a logical choice for a man who might want to shoot waterfowl on the banks of the river seen in the background, which looks very much like the Hudson.

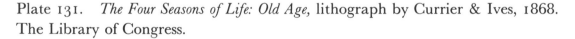

THE FOUR SEASONS OF LIFE: OLD AGE.

Plate 131. *The Four Seasons of Life: Old Age,* lithograph by Currier & Ives, 1868. The Library of Congress.

This is another credible interior based on the work of J. M. Ives. The kerosene lamp has appeared and sits upon a doily on the covered center table. In front of the fire is a hearth rug on top of the wall-to-wall carpeting. Looking upwards there are candlesticks on the mantel which are now only decorations, and they share the space with seashells and a vase. Peacock feathers, along with seashells a Victorian delight, lie above the mirror. This mirror, like the pictures, is hung at an angle from the wall on long wires that quite probably go up to a picture molding near the ceiling. The window has both drapes and lacy glass curtains that depend from behind an embossed and gilded brass valance and are tied with ornamental ropes to fancy tie-backs. The mood of coziness is enhanced by the slipcover on the armchair, and a final detail of interest is added by the cylindrical cushion on the sofa behind it.

Plate 132. "Diagram for Setting a Table," woodcut from *The American Agriculturist*, February 1869. Courtesy Vera Craig.

"There are two things necessary to the proper enjoyment of a meal, whatever or wherever it may be: these are order and scrupulous neatness," wrote *The American Agriculturist*. And it went on to state that "The table should be set as nearly as possible in the same way, so that those who eat at it will always know where to look for whatever they require." With these thoughts in mind, the writer specified that the meat and carving utensils should always be placed before the man while the soup should be stationed before the lady although he was "well aware that soup is not frequently served at farmers' tables. . . ." Four vegetables were somewhat more than usual, but he recommended that when fewer were used they should be placed before the older members of the family. A spoon should be placed upon the table for each dish to be served and there should also be one or two to spare. If individual salts were to be used, then individual saltspoons would not be necessary, but with only two salts the writer recommended special spoons. Dessert should be placed on a side table if there were no servants. Thus would a well-bred farmer (and probably a city dweller as well) set his table at mid century. Perhaps it is because of the possibility of soup, but it should be noted that this is the first picture thus far discovered that indicates a spoon for each setting. Previously a knife and fork had been deemed enough for most dinners.

DIAGRAM FOR SETTING A TABLE.

Plate 133. *The Panic of 1869* attributed to Charles Knoll, oil, 1869. Colby College Art Museum.

The artist, whether Knoll or not, was somewhat less than an expert draftsman. Proportions and perspective have eluded him here and there, but he still conveys an accurate feeling of a cluttered mid-Victorian interior. There is a very unusual lamp (kerosene?) on the marble-top table, and the gas chandelier in the back room looks as if it may be adjustable via double pulleys. The lace antimacassar on the distressed financier's chair has reached its full development, but most interesting, perhaps, is the row of fringe along the front of the hearth. It lies with the free ends back over the carpet instead of on the hearth as one would normally expect.

Plate 134. *Cadet John B. Kerr in his quarters at West Point,* photograph, c. 1868–1869. Courtesy the West Point Museum.

Military men also had homes—of sorts. Here the cadet quarters present interesting contrasts. The bare floors and spartan cots with their stacked bedding contrast with the opulent curtains with valances and tassels and the decorative covers on the work tables. Apparently each cadet could select his own table covering and his own coverlet since the two sets in this room differ. He also placed his own toilet articles on either side of the communal washbasin on the stand. Here, both the top and the shelf of the stand are covered with white cloths, the lower one holding one of the two wooden buckets for wash water. The room is so cold that one almost instinctively thinks of winter yet the work table at the right is pressed directly against the fireplace opening. In winter it must have been moved farther into the room.

Plate 135. *Robert E. Lee in his Study, Washington College* by Adalbert J. Volck, oil, 1870. Courtesy the Valentine Museum, Richmond.

Another military man who had been a West Point cadet spent his final days in much less spartan quarters, A. J. Volck visited Lee at Lexington, Virginia, while he was president of Washington college and made the sketches from which this painting was done just a few months before Lee's death. A chromolithograph was later based upon it. Here Lee seems to have appropriated some old dining room furniture for his purposes. The sideboard holding books and papers on the right is a fine Empire piece, and the round pedestal table with its red cloth looks like a dining room piece despite the litter lying upon it. A laundry basket serves for wastepaper. There is a map on the wall, and another map lies upon the old trunk behind the sideboard. Few museum curators would have the courage to furnish a study with such obviously inappropriate pieces today, but the evidence is still here, corroborated by four photographs taken shortly after Lee's death. They show the same furniture, but without the maps, the trunk, and much of the debris that accumulates in an actively used room.

Plate 136. *The Music Lesson* by George Brown, oil, c. 1870. The Metropolitan Museum of Art; gift of Colonel Charles A. Fowler, 1921.

The flute may have been uppermost in the mind of the musically inclined young lady, but there are other definite overtones in this wealthy Victorian interior. The Victorian Renaissance sofa is of the best quality, and the appointments generally suggest the best taste of the period. A fringed throw rug protects the carpet in front of the sofa, and the heavy drapes are caught with ropes and tassels. The edge of lace glass curtains peek from behind. The growing plants in the pot on the brass stand, and even the vine in the tiny vase on a bracket right in the midst of the pictures on the wall reflect the increased interest in bringing growing things into the home.

Plate 137. *Rococo Parlor* by an unknown artist, oil, c. 1870. Courtesy the New York State Historical Association.

Some pictures of American interiors pose more questions than they answer, and this intriguing primitive is a prime example. It was found in Orrington, Maine, in the possession of a seafaring family, and it is presumed to represent a home in that area. But what sort of a room is it? There is a large table with a huge compote of fruit, suggesting a dining room, but the chairs are not dining room chairs, and they are too few in number. Also the room appears to be on at least the second floor. The books and papers on the table suggest that perhaps this was a parlor—or even a meeting room when one considers the Masonic devices on the ceiling. The bare room beyond the door on the right also evokes a public use image in contrast to the governess, children and cat which are strongly domestic. In any event, there are some interesting design features, especially the panels on the walls and ceilings with their overall pattern of diamonds with floral centers. One wonders if these are wallpaper, damask, or even frosted glass, for the painting shows them in a silvery gray. The wall below the chair rail has been marbleized, and the floors of the front and back room are carpeted while the hall appears to be tiled. It is an expensive building, opulently decorated, but very much of a mystery.

Plate 138. *Merritt Art Gallery, Lyndhurst*, photograph, c. 1870. Collection of Mrs. Alan Douglas Merritt, courtesy the National Trust for Historic Preservation.

Alexander Jackson Davis, the great exponent of the Gothic Revival style in America, designed Lyndhurst in 1838 as a country retreat on the banks of the Hudson River for Congressman William Paulding. In 1864 George Merritt purchased the house and enlarged it under the direction of the original architect. This is the combination billiard room and art gallery as it appeared during the Merritt residence. Originally it had been Paulding's library. The paintings are crammed together on every available space in typical Victorian style. Four of them even hang on the great shuttered window at the end. Seldom have billiard players enjoyed such artistic surroundings. Davis designed the Gothic style chairs along the walls especially for Lyndhurst.

Fortunately a number of photographs survive that illustrate great American mansions of this period. Another exceptionally good collection shows the Lockwood-Matthews house in Norwalk, Connecticut. They were taken about 1868–1872 and have been published in the March 1970 issue of *Antiques*. Lyndhurst is a property of the National Trust for Historic Preservation and is open to the public.

Plate 139. *Gothic Drawing Room, Lyndhurst*, photograph, c. 1870. Collection of Mrs. Alan Douglas Merritt, courtesy the National Trust for Historic Preservation.

Alexander Jackson Davis originally designed Gothic style furniture to complement the architecture in this room also. Here, however, the Merritts have substituted furnishings in the later rococo fashion.

Plate 140. *Merritt Reception Room, Lyndhurst,* photograph, c. 1870. Collection of Mrs. Alan Douglas Merritt, courtesy the National Trust for Historic Preservation.

Here the Merritts have used a mixture of mid-century furniture styles in a room that still retains the Gothic architecture of Davis' designs. Interesting details include the murals on the ceiling and the parquet floor softened by a throw rug in front of the settee. There is also a fitted cloth cover on the grand piano.

Plate 141.   *Merritt Library, Lyndhurst,* photograph c. 1870. Collection of Mrs. Alan Douglas Merritt, courtesy the National Trust for Historic Preservation.

Again, the Merritts have superimposed furniture of a number of styles on the Gothic interior. An interesting but barely visible detail is the small work lamp suspended below the gas chandelier to provide light for the desk. A clearer picture of such a light appears in plate 143. The striped slipcovers with their ruffled skirts on the armchairs suggest that this may be a summer scene.

CHRISTMAS IN THE SOUTH—EGG-NOG PARTY.—[Drawn by W. L. Sheppard.]

Plate 142. "Christmas in the South", woodcut after a drawing by William L. Sheppard, from *Harper's Weekly*, December 31, 1870. Courtesy the Valentine Museum, Richmond.

Sheppard was a careful delineator of Virginia scenes, making almost a fetish of accuracy. In this convivial gathering as guests enjoy eggnog and music, the people almost blot out the room itself. Still, some useful details come through. Not the least of these is the technique of preparing the eggnog in the living room directly in a punch bowl and serving it in glass tumblers. The tables with their cloths seem to have been moved into the room specifically for this purpose, and there is no obvious sign of Christmas greenery. The armchair at the left is fitted with a striped slipcover exactly similar to those shown at Lyndhurst, indicating the widespread popularity of the style. And this is definitely a winter scene.

Plate 143. *The Family of Alfredrick Smith Hatch in their Residence at Park Avenue and 37th Street, New York City* by Eastman Johnson, oil, 1871. The Metropolitan Museum of Art; gift of Frederick H. Hatch, 1926.

Eastman Johnson's paintings ranged from the very simple interiors of Plates 127 and 128 to this highly sophisticated and expensive room in New York City. Here the grand design called for a carpet that seems to have been woven especially to fit and a great cornice over the windows with the family monogram in the center. Two windows have the lace glass curtains dropping straight to cover the windows completely, but the one on the left has the curtains pulled back to show a wreath, suggesting that this is the Christmas season. Slight doubts about the time of year, however, are raised by the greenery on the center table and the fact that the fireplace opening seems to be filled with a screen. Just below the gas chandelier is a separate lamp that can quite probably be lowered to offer a direct working light on the table surface. It is another version of the desk lamp at Lyndhurst shown in place 141.

Plate 144. *The William H. Vanderbilt Family* by Seymour J. Guy, oil, 1873. Courtesy of Biltmore House & Gardens, Asheville, N. C.

When Seymour Guy painted this group portrait of the Vanderbilts in their New York City home they had not yet become the fabulously wealthy clan into which they would soon develop. Still, this was the library of a very well-to-do family of the period. They could afford special painted designs in the coves of the ceiling and decorative painted borders at the ceiling and just above the chair rail. They collected art, and hung their paintings in profusion on all walls. And the assemblage of objets d'art on the mantel and adjoining bookcase is both eclectic and prolific. Interesting details include the special shaded desk lamp hung on the gas chandelier but directing its light downward, and the standing newspaper and magazine rack at the left. Colorwise the whole room is keyed to red, yellow and brown. The walls are yellow; the trim is red and brown as is the carpet. The drapes and upholstery are red. And, of course, the rich reddish brown of the woodwork blends well with the whole.

Plate 145. *Library of the Henry Blow Residence,* photograph, c. 1875. Missouri Historical Society.

Henry Blow built his handsome home in St. Louis in 1859, and, according to general belief, the arrangement and decoration of his library remained unchanged until after this photograph was taken about 1875. Even careful scrutiny can detect no regional difference that distinguished this Mid-western room from those of similar opulence on the East Coast. The dark carved woodwork, the decorated cove of the ceiling and the murals on the ceiling proper represent almost universal features. So does the gas chandelier with its desk light below. The bracket lamp on the wall, however, seems to burn kerosene rather than gas. Mr. Blow's personal taste, though, does seem to have been somewhat different from the Vanderbilts'. At least his mantel supports only a sculptural clock, and there are none of the miscellaneous objets d'art that characterized the Vanderbilt library.

Plate 146. *Boy by a Stove* by Charles C. Markham, oil, 1873. Courtesy Kennedy Galleries, Inc., New York City.

Markham restricted the scope of his composition to a very small portion of a Victorian living room, but he managed to illustrate many features of winter life in a middle class home. Next to the boy, the stove is the subject of greatest prominence, and the artist has included all the pertinent details. This model has the cooking top available and in use for heating the teakettle. The other end of the stove rests upon a metal plate with a whiskbroom handy for cleaning up any spilled ashes or coal dirt. The coal scuttle and shovel also sit nearby. The old fireplace has been closed in, and the pipe from the stove passes through the new fireboard to use the old flue. The carpet is a cheap striped variety, but even this has been protected in front of the stove with a fluffy throw rug. Care and comfort speak from every inch of the picture.

Plate 147. *The Earring* by Eastman Johnson, oil, 1873. In the collection of the Corcoran Gallery of Art; gift of Capt. A. S. Hickey in memory of his wife, Caryl Crawford Hickey.

In this fascinating interior the literal Eastman Johnson offers several useful bits of information as well as a couple of enigmas. Among the latter is the purpose of the room. It is a downstairs room, and the handsome Hepplewhite sideboard with the case of bottles suggests that it is a dining room. Yet the covered hassock and the footstool are not normally items of dining room equipment; and the sewing basket on the left top of the sideboard is also a bit unusual. The geranium in the pot on the windowsill and the vine in the tureen on the sideboard are instructive, as is the sketch that seems to be tacked on the wall next to the mirror. The portiere at left is an early representation of a very important feature of the last part of the century. The wallpaper appears above the chair rail only, and there is a separate border at the ceiling. Most important of all, however, is the window treatment. The drapes have been removed, leaving only the valance, which suggests that this is probably a summer scene. Also, there is a rolled shade of slats of the type that is still used on porches today. This is one of the very few instances in which such a shade is illustrated in a formal room.

Plate 148. *Conversation Group of Baltimore Girls* by Henry Bebie, oil, c. 1873–1875. The Peale Museum, Baltimore.

Not every house is a home, and many viewers who have examined this painting have expressed grave doubts about the propriety of this domicile. Their mental reservations have been caused by the number of young ladies, all of approximately the same age, which would rule out a family group. It might be a fancy female academy, but the central figure in deshabille with an officer in the uniform of the 1870's visible through the open door and a second chap (who can be glimpsed in the mirror) peering through another door do not seem to accord with proper Victorian decorum. Nevertheless there are some pertinent details of domestic decorative practices that the single-minded viewer can discover. The draping of the dressing table mirror in silk or lace is a technique that Bebie has documented in another Baltimore painting now in a private collection, as is the use of a full cloth cover on the table itself. And the covering of the taller footstool in two different fabrics plus a row of fringe is also a significant bit of information.

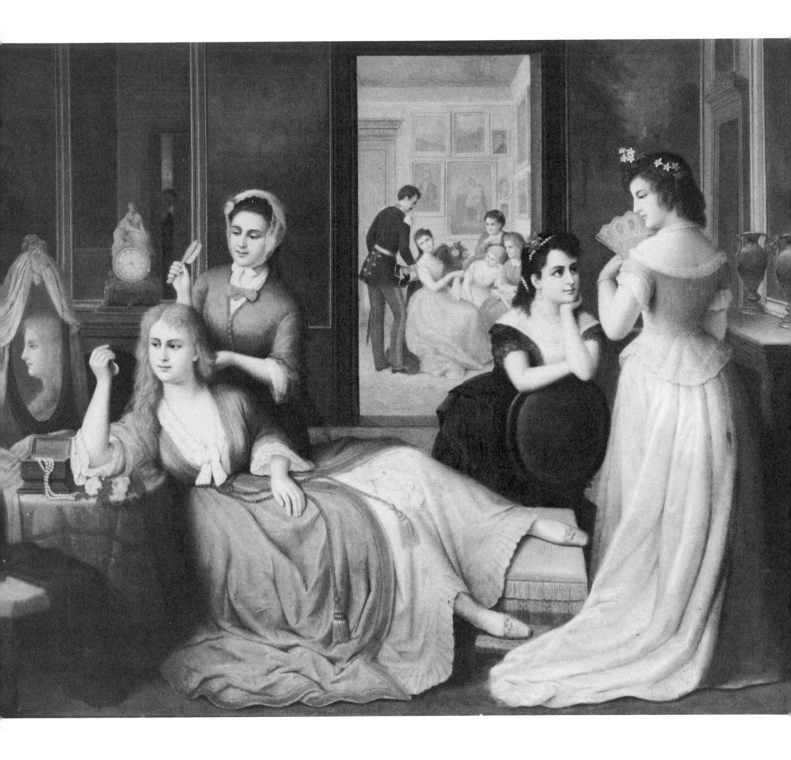

Plate 149. *Child in the Sitting Room* by Ella Emory, oil, c. 1870–1875. Collection of Bertram K. and Nina Fletcher Little.

Sometime in the early to mid 1870's Ella Emory posed her niece on the Empire sofa in the west sitting room of the 17th century Peter Cushing House in Hingham, Massachusetts, and created this record of an early room with overlays from several later periods. The old walls now support wallpaper above the chair rail with a border at the ceiling, and the changing taste added a corner cupboard in the 18th century. There is a roller shade but no drapes or curtains on the window while a separate cushion on the seat formed by the thick old walls provides comfort for two kittens. A white fur rug protects the carpet in front of the sofa, and a fluffy doily separates the columnar lamp from the top of the spool table. The banjo clock sits on a very Victorian wall bracket instead of hanging on the wall, but perhaps the most interesting detail is a small one, very difficult to see in a reproduction. A close examination of the two prints that flank the mirror shows that they have been mounted with window mats! It has been almost a tenet of faith that mats like these had not come into use at this date, but the painting itself leaves no doubt that they were on these pictures.

Plate 150. *Chamber in the Peter Cushing House* by Ella Emory, oil, 1878. Collection of Bertram K. and Nina Fletcher Little.

The date that Ella Emory painted this room portrait falls just a trifle after the period covered in this volume. Yet it is obvious that almost nothing in the room had been changed for many years. The fourposter bed even retains its 18th century hangings. The wing chair and desk also date from that century, but the slipcover on the chair is quite probably about 1850, and the desk has been graced with a long white runner in mid 19th century style. The floor is covered with strips of straw matting, and these, too, have very probably been there for many years. On top of the matting in front of the desk is a braided rug. Such rugs are known from documentary references and from surviving examples, but this is one of the very few contemporary pictures that show one in use. Another small rug lies by the left side of the bed. The small pedestal table may be another old piece of furniture, or it may possibly be the newest one in the room. The long cloth covers so much of it that one cannot be sure. On its top is a fallen vase holding what appear to be two dahlias, knocked over by the playful cat that hides behind one of the folds of the tablecloth.

Plate 151. *The East Parlor of the Peter Cushing House* by Ella Emory, oil, 1878. Collection of Bertram K. and Nina Fletcher Little.

Again Ella Emory skillfully depicts the Victorian overlay in a fine 17th century house. Here the floor is bare except for a hearth rug of large dimensions. This is probably not a case of the carpet having been taken up for the summer because there is a fire in the fireplace, and a shawl thrown over the fancy late Windsor chair, both of which suggest colder weather. The Boston rocker has a separate cushion on the seat with a long cover that is thrown up over the top of the back. Such a back cover could also help keep off drafts. The decorations on the mantel, the newspaper rack on the wall, the bellows, etc., are all eminently Victorian. Incidentally, the Cushing House still stands, and many of the furnishings illustrated in these three paintings are still in it, often in different rooms now than they were when the artist recorded them.

Plate 152. *Wash House* by Ella Emory, oil, c. 1878. Collection of Bertram K. and Nina Fletcher Little.

The last of this series of room pictures by Ella Emory shows the interior of the wash house or laundry that used to serve the Peter Cushing House. During the restoration of the house in 1945 it was moved to the east end where it now serves as a kitchen. Few people bothered to record such mundane rooms as garrets or wash houses so this little painting done on a brass stove hole plate is a very welcome document. There is the usual Windsor chair that has lost its back at the far right and a very early hutch table on the left. Perhaps of greatest interest is the rolled blind of slats on the window which works very much like some in use today.

Plate 153. *Deacon Jones' Experience* by Archibald M. Willard, oil, 1874. Allen Memorial Art Museum, Oberlin College.

Here Archibald Willard portrays a probably fictional setting in a home of a family of very modest means. Still, they have a striped carpet of less than room size on the unpainted wooden floor, and the table is covered with a white table-cloth. The chairs are very late Windsor types, and the one in the foreground is yellow with painted decorations. Through the doorway a bed can be seen with the pillows on top of the coverlet in typical fashion for the period. The cause of all the trouble is a young pug. This seems a somewhat esoteric breed for the family, but obviously the artist had seen such an animal despite the fact that the breed books say the pug was first introduced to this country in the 1880's.

Plate 154. *Interior of Sawtell's Ranch at Henry Lake,* photograph by William H. Jackson, 1872. Courtesy the U. S. Geological Survey.

When W. H. Jackson visited the Sawtell Ranch in Fremont County, Idaho, he described the simple ranch house as "very comfortable quarters." The ranchers themselves sit in the foreground on a box and a rough version of a captain's chair. The other three men were members of the survey expedition. The walls are wood, quite probably squared logs. Guns—muzzle-loaders, Sharps and Spencer carbines plus Remington and Colt revolvers, most of them dating from the Civil War—dominate the room. Here, for the first time in a contemporary picture, the guns are on and around the mantel. Perhaps by 1872 reality had caught up with the legend of the gun over the fireplace.

Plate 155. "Sod House—Interior," woodcut from *The American Agriculturist,* May 1874. Courtesy Vera Craig.

In such areas as Nebraska and its neighboring states where timber was scarce, the settlers lived in houses of sod, using the valuable wood only for doors, window frames and roof supports. The majority of the photographs of these sod houses which survive date from the 1880's and 1890's, but here an artist from *The American Agriculturist* portrays one of the dwellings in which some of the paper's subscribers lived. In commenting on the house, the paper stated, "Books, pictures, and music are sometimes seen in such habitations. . . . In the interiors of some such houses as the one here pictured, well-filled bookshelves, a musical instrument, newspapers and magazines may be seen, and yet the floor may be of earth and the chimney of sticks plastered with mud." With a dirt floor the stove did not require a metal plate or box of sand for fire protection. Yet it is interesting to note that there is a throw rug at the door to prevent more dirt being carried in. In the door also is a board that makes the threshold high enough to keep out chickens and other livestock, though the cat, at least, seems to have been able to get over it. There was even one mistress of a sod house, the writer reported, who declared she would much rather make do with a dirt floor than do without her subscription to *The American Agriculturist!*

SOD HOUSE—INTERIOR.

Plate 156. "Wash Stand and Bathtub," woodcut from *The American Agriculturist,* May 1874. Courtesy Vera Craig.

Few modern Americans raised to inside plumbing can remember when the wash stand was a fixture in every bedroom. *The American Agriculturist,* however, commemorated this shrine of cleanliness on its cover in 1874 and thus provided an excellent documentation of its appearance. Here a Sheraton style stand holds the water pitcher, wash bowl, soap dish and toothbrush in a paneled tumbler on its top shelf, a brush, comb, and probably a box of hair pins, etc., below. A mirror hangs above, and at the left are a towel rack and a covered slop basin while a tin bathtub that only occasionally entered the bedroom (on Saturday nights!) stands in front. The other object is a bit hard to identify. If it is a sponge, it is certainly one of the biggest ever seen.

Plate 157. *Party at the Custers',* photograph c. 1875. Custer Battlefield National Monument.

For most of their married lives General and Mrs. George Armstrong Custer lived in Army quarters. Here they have gathered some of their relatives and other friends for an afternoon's festivities in their home at Fort Abraham Lincoln, Dakota Territory. Custer himself stands by the piano. His wife, Elizabeth, sits pensively behind him, her head against her hand. The chandelier and bracket lamp with its reflector are kerosene, since gas would not have been available on the frontier. Here a birdcage hangs beneath the chandelier, and the paintings hang on long wires from a picture molding. The Douglas chair at the left documents the presence of a type that has long been popularly associated with the West. The chair or sofa behind it is dim, but obviously slipcovered in a plain fabric with ruffles that reach the floor. This must be a summer or late spring scene because there is a small bouquet on the piano.

Plate 158. *Interior, Custers' Quarters*, photograph, c. 1875. Custer Battlefield National Monument.

This photograph was taken from almost the same angle as the preceding one, but someone, undoubtedly Mrs. Custer, has moved everything around. The piano now stands in front of the fireplace which has been closed with a fireboard. This instrument was an important part of the Custer lives. They complained about the difficulties of hauling the piano from post to post, but they would not do without it. Here an Indian blanket which does not appear in the other photograph lies across it. The birdcage has been removed from its place below the chandelier, and there is a covered ottoman or footstool alongside the piano. The Rogers groups, however, still stand on the mantel. Here one can clearly see the dining room beyond with its striped tablecloth and separate carpet.

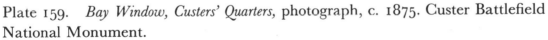

Plate 159.   *Bay Window, Custers' Quarters*, photograph, c. 1875. Custer Battlefield National Monument.

The Custers firmly subscribed to the 1870 attitude which called for converting the home into a veritable greenhouse of growing plants and vines. This scene was quite probably taken at the same time as the one shown in the preceding plate. Here one finds the birdcage moved from its cold weather spot beneath the chandelier to a sunnier location in the bay window. The terraced plant stand is similar to the one placed next to the piano, and here, at last, one can detect the pattern in the carpet which burned out completely in the other two photographs. The guitar reflects the Custers' interest in music once again. There is a lace antimacassar on the chair in proper Victorian style, and one can make out at least some suggestion of the lace glass curtains and drapes which Elizabeth Custer hung across the base of the bay.

Plate 160. *General and Mrs. Custer at Fort Abraham Lincoln,* photograph, c. 1875. Custer Battlefield National Monument.

Here is an entirely different room from those shown in the preceding three pictures. It quite probably served as a study or library. The walls are papered and decorated with a stuffed owl, game heads, military and hunting equipment and portraits of Custer himself and his Civil War commander Phil Sheridan. In the right corner is a circular gun rack holding both long and hand guns, but the center of interest is the table. On it rest a student lamp and the same two Rogers groups that appear on the mantel in the previous pictures of the living room. Custer had a special fondness for these groups. Because of the hardships of wagon transportation these plaster sculptures frequently suffered, and Custer himself carefully patched and repainted them each time they broke. Another interesting feature is the thermometer that hangs on the wall just above the lamp.

Plate 161. *Detail, Custers' Quarters*, photograph, c. 1875. Custer Battlefield National Monument.

Looking at this scene one wonders if the Custers actually used this grouping or whether they arranged it especially for the photograph. The gun rack seems to be the same one shown in the previous plate. The Rogers group has already appeared in two previous locations (on the living room mantel, on the study table, and on this pedestal). In any event it depicts a possible composition for hunting equipment and trophies plus military gear.

Plate 162. "Sleeping Room of the Men Shakers," woodcut from a sketch by J. Becker from *Frank Leslie's Illustrated Newspaper*, September 6, 1873. Courtesy Marius B. Peladeau.

Among the very specialized homes in America were those of the various religious and utopian communities, including those of the sexually segregated Shakers who designed and produced some of the most efficiently satisfying furniture and utensils in the country. In this view of the sleeping quarters of the Shaker men at Mount Lebanon, New York, the artist illustrates several aspects of special interest. The stove, for instance, is a Shaker design with a heat chamber above the firebox for the more efficient utilization of the hot air. The beds have wheels so that they can be moved easily for the women to perform their daily cleaning chores. The walls at left are draped with a checked cloth hung from the rack of pegs. At the right the wall is bare with a brush and a flat broom—another Shaker invention—hanging from these pegs. The floor is covered with strips of matting. In the summer this was a grass or straw matting which was replaced in winter by narrow woven carpeting. Since a supply of firewood sits ready in a basket by the door, this may well be a winter scene with carpeting rather than grass or straw. It is impossible to tell from Becker's sketch. The stove rests on a slab of hard wood, probably maple. It is an ascetic room, but not without comfort—or at least a rocking chair.

SLEEPING-ROOM OF THE MEN SHAKERS.
THE SHAKERS OF LEBANON, NEW YORK.—Sketched by J. Becker.

THE KITCHEN OF THE CHURCH FAMILY.

THE SHAKERS OF LEBANON, NEW YORK.—SKETCHED BY J. BECKER.

Plate 163. "The Kitchen of the Church Family," woodcut from a sketch by J. Becker from *Frank Leslie's Illustrated Newspaper*, September 13, 1873. Courtesy Marius B. Peladeau.

In the Shaker communities the women performed the cooking duties in a functional and efficient kitchen. Most of the utensils shown are quite probably tinned iron, made by the Shaker men. The stove is probably an item of purchase from the outside world, and it appears to sit on a sheet of metal rather than the hardwood slab that the Shakers often used. Otherwise the floor is bare just as it was in almost every other kitchen across the land. The water that the cooks could pump into the sink came from a reservoir on a hill, from which it flowed by gravity through a refrigerator room before it could be tapped for kitchen use.

Plate 164. *The Kitchen* by Louis Prang, chromolithograph by L. Prang & Co., 1874. The Library of Congress.

By 1874 the ideal American kitchen had progressed mightily. Louis Prang could illustrate for his teaching series a fully equipped food preparation center with an iron coal range connected to a hot water tank. Nearby is a sink with hot and cold running water, though there is still a wooden slop bucket standing next to it. The floor is of plain wood, but a tile hearth affords safety from fire beneath the stove. On the hearth sits the coal scuttle with its small shovel, and on the other side lie two of the stove lids that have been removed from beneath a couple of the iron cooking kettles. Against the brick chimney front on the left rest the essential tools for coal stove operation: a whisk broom and dustpan for cleaning up ashes and coal dust, a poker, a wrench for shaking down the ashes, and a lifter for removing hot stove lids. The wall clock is a spring type, and the roller towel at the extreme right is of a type that was still common in American country kitchens until World War II. Barely visible in the windows at each side are spring roller shades with painted or printed designs. Finally, here is a good picture of what a well-arranged kitchen cupboard might have contained—if the cook had been an artist like Mr. Prang!

PUBLISHED BY L. PRANG & Cº BOSTON.

THE KITCHEN

COPYRIGHT, 1874, BY L. PRANG & C

Plate 165. *Charles Sumner's House, Looking from Dining Room to Library*, photograph, c. 1875. Courtesy Smithsonian Institution.

Anna Dickinson visited Senator Sumner's home in Washington some time before his death in 1874. With a sensitive woman's eye she viewed the great Abolitionist's cluttered rooms and recorded her impressions in her later book *A Ragged Register:*

> His house was too small for the treasures he had collected. The hall, on the one hand opening into the drawing-room, on the other to the library and dining room, and the stairway of black walnut were papered by rare engravings.
>
> Below, the rooms, connected by folding doors, had the expansive effect of one noble apartment. At the right, the drawing-room, showing a lovely Wilton carpet, its chief color an exquisite blue, the curtains and hangings a delicate amber. The pictures, masterpieces, all save one—a freak of his—the chromo of Whittier's "Barefoot Boy." . . .
>
> On one side, the library-doors crowded with engravings of horses and horses' heads. "I never owned a horse," said he, "but here is my stable. Who can equal it?" The other side was covered with likenesses of the most famous gateways and doorways, ancient and modern.
>
> The walls and mantle packed with curious and beautiful bronzes and paintings, even the floor about the walls, supporting pictures that else could find no resting-place. Indeed the room was so overcrowded with beauty as to lose beauty, but the dining-room was perfection, the colors so rich as to be fruity, a Turkish table-cover, wonderful glass and china, and carved things and superb paintings all in absolute harmony.
>
> His study, his "den" as he called it, always interested me, as it must have interested any one who had the happiness to enter it, more than any other room in the house. At the head of the stairway, on the second floor, adjoining his sleeping-room, heaped and jammed with books and papers, on tables, chairs, the floor itself with scarce space for one to turn. Here he really lived, and you, who looked at it, realized what a hard worker was its master.
>
> Here he had gathered the rarest collection of framed engravings in America, the careful accumulation of a lifetime. In this country no one else owned such portraits and proofs, many of them carrying the autograph of both painter and engraver.

This and the following photographs of the Sumner home were taken by Washington photographer D. R. Holmes after the Senator's death as part of a stereoscopic series.

Plate 166. *Charles Sumner's House, Looking from the Library to the Dining Room*, photograph, c. 1875. Courtesy Smithsonian Institution.

Flanking the library door are two busts, one of the Senator himself (left) and Julius Caesar (right). Beyond the door is the dining room which Anna Dickinson described as "perfection." The "wonderful" glass and china must have been removed from the sideboard and wall brackets, and the Turkish tablecover is hardly discernible, but at least the "superb" paintings still hang on the walls. Interestingly, all of the pictures in Sumner's home seem to have been hung on blind cords at a time when long visible cords were usual. Perhaps there just wasn't room on the Senator's crowded walls to expose them.

Plate 167. *Charles Sumner's Study,* photograph, c. 1875. Courtesy Smithsonian Institution.

The "den" where Sumner "really lived" has obviously been cleaned since his death. The strewn books and papers that covered desk and floor have largely disappeared, though enough remain to give the room a lived-in look. The desk in the foreground had originally been designed by Thomas U. Walter, Architect of the Capitol, for the House of Representatives. Sumner bought two of these desks at auction in 1873 and installed them in his study. Another interesting aspect of the furnishings are the two distinct sets that have been combined in one room. Each set consists of a sofa, at least one armchair and several side chairs. Apparently the Senator made no attempt to relate the two sets to each other. Even the upholstery material remains different. The gas desk lamp is an unusual pattern with a statuary base, but it is fueled in the common manner with a rubber hose to the chandelier above.

Plate 168. *Charles Sumner's Drawing Room,* photograph, c. 1875. Courtesy Smithsonian Institution.

In sharp contrast to the cluttered study, the drawing room or parlor enjoyed a formal and elegant appearance with a strong inclination to the new French Renaissance revival style. Typical is the center ottoman beneath the fine crystal gas chandelier, and the corners of the two Renaissance style chairs with Pompeian legs that intrude slightly at each edge of the picture. The walls here are papered rather than painted like the others in the house. There is an elaborate gilded cornice over the fringed valance of the heavy cut velvet (?) drapes that hide the lace glass curtains, and the closed shutters offer an interesting detail. They have four vertically louvered panels to let in some light and air while maintaining privacy. The statue is "Venus in the Bath."

Plate 169. *Charles Sumner's Drawing Room,* photograph, c. 1875. Courtesy Smithsonian Institution.

Taken from the window alcove, this view of the drawing room is almost directly opposite the one just preceding. Venus is in the foreground, and there is a better view of the center ottoman that shows the central support for the cushions and the braided rope around the base. On the wall at the right is a three-back divan with a similar rope. All the major upholstered pieces have matching fabric. The white marble fireplace supports a gilt French clock with cherubim and a large mirror with gilt moldings also in the Renaissance style. And, of course, paintings abound on all available wall space.

Plate 170. *Charles Sumner's Bedroom*, photograph, c. 1875. Courtesy Smithsonian Institution.

Compared with the other rooms in the house, the Senator's bedroom is almost a model of simplicity. There are relatively few engravings on the walls, and the woodwork is painted to match the wall color. The cheval mirror and the bed are of fine quality and in the Renaissance style, but one can only guess about the marble-topped washstand and dresser.

Plates 171 & 172. *Library of the William N. Byers Residence,* photograph, April 1874 Denver Public Library Western Collection. Photos by Chamberlain.

These two photographs show most of the library of the Byers home at the corner of Sherman and Colfax in Denver, Colorado. There are no drapes or curtains, an unusual circumstance for this season of the year, and the following photographs of the parlor suggest there were none in any of the major rooms of the house. Instead, the folding shutters with their louvered panels provided privacy with ventilation. Bilateral symmetry seems to have prevailed in decoration, although the upholstered chairs and sofa have individual and distinctive antimacassars. The furniture is generally in the Renaissance style, and here the desire for greenery has degenerated into artificial leaves to transform the picture wires into vines plus bouquets of ferns and Pampas grass in the scattered vases.

Plates 173 & 174. *Parlor of the William N. Byers Residence,* photographs, April 1875. Denver Public Library Western Collection. Photos by Chamberlain.

These two views offer complementary glimpses of Mr. Byers' Denver parlor which was also generally in the Renaissance style. Again there is some fake greenery and some Pampas grass, but the vine trained over the archway may be entirely real. In the alcove beyond is a conservatory with a multitude of growing plants and a birdcage mounted on a wall bracket. The interesting kerosene lamp on the center table rests in a circle of artificial (?) bunches of purple and white grapes. In the second photograph the lamp and grapes have been removed, and the piano has been turned and moved slightly. False greenery surrounds the two pictures in the bay window, and a very interesting cluster of balls or bells hangs from the ceiling to form an exceptionally early mobile.

Plate 175. *Living Room of the Dr. J. G. Bailey Home, Santa Ana, California,* photograph, c. 1876. Courtesy Charles W. Bowers Memorial Museum, Santa Ana.

Officials at the Bowers Museum have good circumstantial evidence which leads them to believe that this photograph was made in 1876. If so, the Baileys were very much up to date, and judging by the quality of the furnishings they could afford to keep abreast of the latest styles. The fireplace boasts tiles of a minstrel in Elizabethan costume and a reclining nude. Bronzes of figures in Renaissance costume and a reproduction broadsword with sculptured hilt (on bookshelf) suggest an admiration for the period of knighthood. The lace glass curtains have an exceptionally deep valance, and they hang straight with no tie-backs. Perhaps the outstanding feature of the room, however, is the marble column surmounted by a sculptural group and surrounded by flowerpots from which spring vines, ferns and other indoor plants. More plants spring from a ginger jar on the table while a pile of cut flowers lie beside it, testifying either to the fertility of southern California or the floraphilia of the Baileys.

Plate 176. *A Family Group* by an unknown artist, watercolor, c. 1875. Courtesy of the Henry Ford Museum, Dearborn, Michigan.

The Victorian family in this rigidly posed group belonged to a far less wealthy segment of society than those whose homes appear in the preceding photographs. The head of the household might well have been a clerk or a skilled craftsman, even a teacher or minister. One of the latter professions is strongly suggested by the books held, the bookcase, and the number of different journals in the newspaper rack on the wall. The furniture is simple; the walls papered with a separate ceiling border, and the woodwork is artificially grained. Everything is good and well cared-for, but nothing is luxurious.

Plate 177. *The Sportsman's Dream* by C. F. Senior, oil, c. 1875. Collection of Edgar William and Bernice Chrysler Garbisch.

Even a cursory examination of this romantic Victorian "den" makes one wonder if the artist had in mind the sentiment expressed by *A Paper of Tobacco* which had appeared in London in 1839:

> How soothing is a pipe to the wearied sportsman on his return to the inn from the moors! As he sits quietly smoking, he thinks of the absent friends whom he will gratify with presents of grouse; and, in a perfect state of contentment with himself and all the world, he determines to give all his game away.

Indeed, the artist, man or woman, seems more familiar with tobacco than with the so-called field sports. The Wellington pipe is accurately portrayed, and the containers of Havana cigars are carefully indicated while the gun and the fishing tackle are completely misunderstood. And the fox which provided the hearth rug must certainly have been one of the largest in creation! Still, it is a cheery masculine interior, comporting well with Victorian coziness.

Plate 178. *Not at Home* by Eastman Johnson, oil, c. 1875. In The Brooklyn Museum
Collection.

Using an old trick, the young lady in Johnson's genre scene dashes upstairs to avoid an
unwelcome visitor. The house is obviously of
mid 19th century vintage, probably New
York City. The furnishings are an eclectic
mixture of the sort that gathers around an
old family. The tall-case clock at the right is
a fine specimen of the late 18th century. The
sofa is a good Sheraton type. But the cupboard, the armchair, and the footstool are
new pieces in the Victorian Elizabethan
form. From an interior decoration standpoint, the most important feature in the
painting is the portiere on a rod that could
close the archway. These curtains became so
popular in the next two decades that in many
instances they did away with interior door-
ways on the ground floor completely.

Plate 179. *Residence of Francisco Bianchi, 61 West 55th St., New York* by James Brownlee Simonson, oil, 1875. Courtesy the Museum of the City of New York.

Far better than the more literal photographs, James Brownlee Simonson has captured the essence of the late Victorian double parlors. Once again the Renaissance style generally prevails in the back parlor which is the focus of the painting. One individualistic feature not shown in any of the other scenes found so far is the white ceramic cuspidor by the fireplace.

Plate 180. *Bedroom, Virginia City, Nevada,* photograph, c. 1875. Courtesy the Nevada Historical Society, Reno.

Nothing is known about this scene except its location. Somehow the appearance seems to suggest a female occupancy, but this is very much in the same category as reading tea leaves. The banner on the door with its Greek letters is an unusual decoration for this part of the country, but the furnishings in general suggest some degree of economic success despite the wainscot ceiling. There is a fur rug beside the bed, and the pillow arrangement is most interesting. Two pillows stand vertically supported by a triangular bolster, and a lace cover lies over the top. The lace coverlet is tucked in at the bottom but hangs free at the sides. At the foot of the bed is a folding chair with three items thrown over the back. The best guess seems to be that they are hand towels with lace borders, but this is open to anyone's interpretation. A second folding chair holds a small laundry bag. One keeps wondering at the significance of this boudoir and why it was photographed since it does not seem to have formed part of a set.

Plate 181. *The Guitar Player* by Frank Buchser, oil, 1867. Courtesy Kennedy Galleries, Inc., New York City.

Painted two years after the close of the Civil War, this is one of the few contemporary pictures to show a Negro living in fairly comfortable quarters. It is a simple room, to be sure, but it appears neat and well maintained, and there are a surprising number of unusual accessories. The shelf above the cupboard on the rear wall holds an impressive array of books, and another book rests on the mantel along with an inkwell and a pen. A folder, scarcely visible behind the chair, is labeled "Melodics," indicating that this guitar player was musically literate as well as talented. The floor is stone, the hearth rug threadbare, the fireplace and cupboard plain, but the atmosphere is one of warmth and contentment.

Plate 182. "Christmas in Virginia: A Present from the Big House," woodcut after a drawing by William L. Sheppard in *Harper's Weekly*, December 30, 1871. Courtesy the Valentine Museum, Richmond.

In stark contrast with the previous plate is this depiction of a Negro home by the Virginia artist William L. Sheppard. Here poverty is emphasized, and students debate whether Sheppard's intentions were patronizing, even if unintentionally so, or whether he meant to contrast this scene with his picture of a gay eggnog party (plate 142) that appeared in the same issue of *Harper's Weekly* in an effort to prod consciences. Be that as it may, Sheppard was normally a keen observer, and he had quite probably seen rough cabins with cloth tacked over windows and fireplaces of sticks and clay. Another interesting detail is the little horseshoe tacked above the fire opening. Too small for real use, even on a pony, it must have been made originally as a good luck decoration such as those currently offered by the blacksmiths at several historical restorations.

Plate 183. *A Virginny Breakdown* by John A. Elder, oil, c. 1875. Courtesy Kennedy Galleries, Inc., New York City.

Another Virginia artist, John Elder, here corroborates some of the details shown in the previous plate by Sheppard. The bare log walls and wooden floor of short boards and the rough batten doors are the same. More intriguing, however, is the fact that both have shown hanging corner cupboards, slat back chairs with rush seats and barrels for storage. The more affluent Guitar Player in plate 181 also had a slat back chair with a rush seat though it was an older one of higher quality. Such unanimity among three separate viewers certainly suggests that these features were common if not almost standard.

Plate 184. *Interior of an Adirondack Shanty* by George B. Wood, Jr., oil, late 1870's. The Adirondack Museum.

Simple northern homes had much in common with those of the Negroes and poorer Whites in the South. Here, George Wood shows a similar batten door, but with two layers of boards, the same bare floor of short boards. Even the chair on which the woman sits seems to be another of the slat back types. As in so many pictures of simple homes, the artist has here caught the dimness of the interior as the occupants work in the light from the open door. Artificial light, whether from candles or oil, cost money and effort, and people used it sparingly. The "shanty" shown here was somewhat unusual in that it had a cellar with a trapdoor opening next to the stove as well as a second floor heated through the circular register cut in the ceiling. The cooking range apparently was too low to suit the taste of the cook, and so it has been placed on a homemade platform to bring it to a more comfortable height. But the most puzzling features of the room are the two rods or pipes suspended just below the ceiling. Running water would have been highly improbable, and so it is quite likely that these are rods for drying. Indeed, a towel is hung over one of them in this picture to give further weight to this theory.

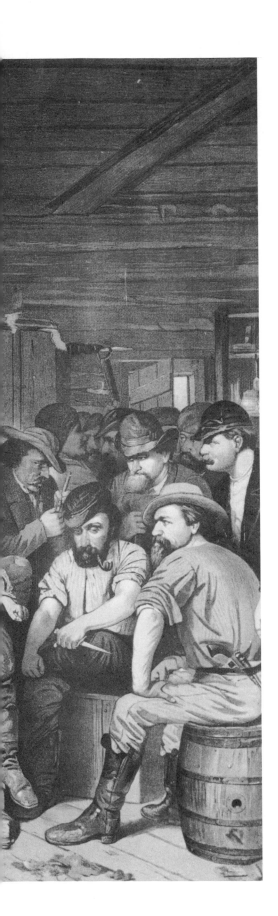

Plate 185. *The Preliminary Trial of an Outlaw,* chromolithograph by Clay Cossack & Co. after a painting by John Milvany, 1877.

The exact nature of the interior portrayed by John Milvany in this picture is not clear. The built-in bed, open and closed cupboards, and various bits of personal gear indicate that the room was indeed used as living quarters. It may well be that the local judge (seated at the table at left) held court in his room, much as Judge Roy Bean held court in his Texas barroom. It is always possible, of course, that the scene is entirely imaginary, designed for Eastern consumption where few people would have had accurate knowledge of rooms and practices in the West. Yet every object in the room has been carefully and accurately drawn, suggesting that the artist paid close attention to physical details. A generally contemporary illustration of an Eastern judge holding court in a cobbler's shop can be seen in *Justice's Court in the Backwoods* painted by Tompkins H. Matteson in 1850 (The New York State Historical Association, Cooperstown).

Plate 186. *Mrs. Martha J. Lamb Seated in Her Library* by Cornelia A. Fassett, oil, 1878. Courtesy of the New-York Historical Society, New York City.

Although Cornelia Fassett painted her delightful portrait of Mrs. Lamb and her library after the close of the stated period for this book, it has been included because it represents the height of aristocratic taste for a city apartment just before the major changes that accompanied the great Centennial Exhibition of 1876. Some wealthy Americans were already acquiring furniture based upon styles associated with colonial America or arranging Oriental corners with screens and vases, but not Mrs. Lamb. True, she has a large Oriental-style vase standing on the floor between the bookcase and the étagère at right, but such vases had appeared well before the Centennial. The folding shutters and lack of curtains or drapes on the window are an unusual feature, but, in general, Mrs. Lamb's library illustrates the epitome of the eclectic mid-Victorian style. As such it is a fitting picture to close this pictorial survey of American domestic interiors from the beginning through the first century of the new United States.

APPENDIX

INN AND TAVERN INTERIORS

While the home remained the center for the lives of most Americans in the years before 1877, the inn and tavern served as a focus for much of their social activity. At least for the men. In the smaller communities and in the residential areas of many cities the inn often functioned much like the neighborhood pub in England. Here men gathered for conversation and perhaps a game of cards or checkers or even billiards. Here, too, they frequently met for more serious purposes. Local committees assembled to cope with crises, to organize for politics or to prepare for defense. Thomas Jefferson and his colleagues set up Virginia's Committee of Correspondence in the Raleigh Tavern at Williamsburg, for instance, and it was there also that the Virginia Burgesses held a rump session to call for a Continental Congress after the Royal Governor had ordered them from the capitol. To the north, Buckman's Tavern in Lexington was a focal point for the Minute Men of Captain John Parker, and many of them sat before the fire in its taproom as they awaited the approach of the British troops in the early morning of April 19, 1775.

The tavern also provided the greatest opportunity for contact with the outside world. Here travelers found lodging; post riders and other messengers stopped for refreshment. They brought with them news of events in other areas, and from there it circulated to the rest of the community. Thoughtful tavernkeepers posted notices of interest, and some even offered newspapers. Stage lines used the local tavern as a stopping point, and in later years the railroads sometimes did too.

In time things changed. From social club and communications center the tavern gradually evolved into a specialized emporium devoted primarily to the sale of beverages to a transient clientele. Lodging and even meal facilities disappeared and the local citizenry found their contacts elsewhere. The inns became hotels, and they too were largely ignored by the residents of the area. It was a slow process, and by 1877 it had occurred only in the larger cities. But the trend was evident. The old-style taverns recorded by William Sidney Mount could still be found in rural areas, but New York already offered such establishments as the Gem Saloon and George Hayward's Porter House, radically different in both appearance and attitude from Lexington's Buckman Tavern in 1775.

Despite the changes over the years, the contemporary pictures clearly indicate some permanent characteristics. Most obvious is the plainness of the taprooms. There are no frills, few fragile furnishings. Floors are plain and easily cleanable. Only two pictures thus far discovered show any floor coverings. George Hayward's Porter House has what appears to be a painted canvas floor cloth, and the Eureka Billiard Hall boasts a rubber mat. Even these would have been easily cleanable. This, after all, is just plain common sense. In a room where all sorts of people would be served food and drink that they might spill and where they would be apt to track in mud, snow and slush, rugs and carpets would soon have been ruined. Delicate furniture and decorative objects could easily be broken by careless or rowdy customers. Few innkeepers would have considered such things worth their cost. Inventories and archeological discoveries at such elite hostelries as the Raleigh Tavern and Henry Wetherburn's in Williamsburg offer proof that some inns had finer and more fragile furnishings, but they were the exceptions that prove the rule. These pictures plus other contemporary views by Mount and Krimmel that have been omitted because they were largely repetitive make it clear that most such establishments were plain and practical. When paintings and curios did become popular for bar decorations, glass cases or high shelves protected them from accidental damage at the hands of possibly exhilarated patrons.

Cuspidors or spitting boxes are prominent throughout, but nowhere is there the traditional brass rail. That still remained for the future.

Plate 187. *Sea Captains Carousing in Surinam* by John Greenwood, oil, 1758. City Art Museum of Saint Louis.

Not even the most jingoistic expansionist has claimed (in recent years, at least) that Surinam is part of the United States. John Greenwood was an American, however, and so, probably, were most of the carousing captains. Also the characteristics of the room agree so closely with later pictures of American inns that it can logically be used as a guide for inns in this country during the middle years of the 18th century. The floor is bare; the furniture is simple and sturdy; and there is a complete absence of daintiness. A looking glass and a clock (along with two hats) adorn the visible walls, but there are no pictures or other decorations. The emphasis is on practicality and "cleanability." The cloth cover on the card table in the rear seems the sole exception to this philosophy. Among the interesting objects shown, one might note the candlestick on the floor with the central drip pan usually associated with the 17th century. Perhaps it was an heirloom, for the other candlesticks are of the Queen Anne-Chippendale styles. Some students have used scenes such as this to "prove" that punch was drunk directly from the bowl, but it seems more likely that the artists have portrayed this to suggest boorishness and vulgarity. Indeed, one of the captains imbibing from a bowl has an upset glass before him, and other pictures of more sedate company illustrate both ladles and glasses along with punch bowls. Behind the bar it is interesting to note that the shelves hold only a few bottles, but that there are extra bowls and two large paper-wrapped loaves of sugar. Wine, brandy and rum, after all, would have been stored in casks with bottles serving a role similar to that of the bowls as service vessels.

Plate 188. *Billiards at a Country Tavern* by Benjamin Latrobe, watercolor, c. 1797.
From the collections of the Maryland Historical Society.

Aside from the barroom, some other rooms in taverns seem to have been stark
and bare. Here the famous architect Latrobe shows a group of local men playing
billiards in a very spartan setting. The floor may have been bare, but it is also
possible that the artist intended to suggest straw matting since he leaves it absolutely plain except for the lines near the center of the table. The windows have
folding shutters but no drapes, and there are no pictures on the walls. Indeed the
first impression is that the room is entirely bare except for the table. A closer look,
however, suggests that the two gentlemen at the left rear are sitting on a high
narrow bench. And some place there must have been a cue rack!

Plate 189. "The York Hotels, Kept in 1800," watercolor from Lewis Miller, *Sketches and Chronicles*. From the Collection of the Historical Society of York County in York, Pennsylvania.

In these two informative sketches Lewis Miller recalls his boyhood experiences and sights in York tavern kitchens. The top scene shows the cook baking bread with the loaf on a wooden peel as she places it in the oven. Iron kettles hang in the fireplace at left, and sausage smokes over a smaller fire at right. It hardly seems likely, however, that she left a plucked chicken lying on the floor! Since Miller discussed Mrs. Hersh's skill in boning a chicken in his notes, he probably felt he should include one in the scene no matter how illogically. The lower sketch shows Lewis himself appreciating a sweet potato fried by Mrs. Lottman in the kitchen of her tavern on South George Street back in 1799. Mrs. Lottman fried sausage and then put the potatoes in the same legged frying pan. A platter rests on the floor next to the hearth to receive the cooked potatoes, and a basket of raw ones stands behind Lewis. To set the scene still further Lewis even includes an exterior view of Mrs. Lottman's establishment.

Plate 190. *Interior of an American Inn* by John Lewis Krimmel, oil, 1813. The Toledo Museum of Art, Toledo, Ohio; Gift of Florence Scott Libbey, 1954.

Krimmel's detailed pictures of American inns are among the very best documents for the appearance of these social centers during the first quarter of the 19th century. In addition to this painting he did another which was engraved by George Lehner with the title *Dance in a Country Tavern*. It may well represent the same inn but adds a gun over the door and a birdcage on the wall. Here the floor is typically bare, but the walls are adorned with a number of prints and posters, some framed, some tacked directly on the wall. Also there is a series of newspapers in wooden holders hanging on nails for the use of patrons. The bar detail is excellent with the shelves holding empty decanters of several sizes, punch bowls, glass tumblers and pewter tankards, a funnel, and boxes that presumably hold sugar and spices. An unusual feature is an office corner at the right with a desk and stool.

Plate 191.   *The Long Story* by William Sidney Mount, oil, 1837. In the collection of the Corcoran Gallery of Art.

Mount described his conversation piece as set in a Long Island tavern with a traveler waiting for the stage, and the tavern keeper sitting on the backless chair in the foreground, adding:

> The principal interest to be centered in the old invalid. . . . I have placed him in a particular chair which he is always supposed to claim by right of possession, being but seldom out of it from the rising to the going down of the sun. A kind of bar-room oracle, . . . and first taster of every new barrel of cider rolled in the cellar, a glass of which he now holds in his hand. . . .

A second point of interest is the stove, set in a box of sand for fire safety, a practice that is documented in many paintings of taverns and schoolrooms of the period. Again the floor, walls, bar and woodwork are plain and unpainted. Tacked-up notices of rail schedules and other information provide the only breaks in the barrenness of decoration.

Plate 192. *Country Inn* attributed to August Kollner, watercolor, 1840. Courtesy Chicago Historical Society.

Presumably this inn was in Pennsylvania since the other watercolors in this series bear notes of locations in that state. (See plate 57.) Here the shelves behind the bar hold an array of bottles in the manner of modern backbars. The floor, walls and bar are all unpainted wood except for the pale blue border on the front of the bar. Decorations consist of snakeskins, a stuffed raccoon, a landscape and notices of public sales tacked on the wall. Charles Dickens noted that the American taverns he visited a few years later almost universally boasted engravings of George Washington and Queen Victoria, but if this fashion had reached rural Pennsylvania by the time of August Kollner's visit, he did not record either of the portraits—unless the lady on the clock face is meant to be the young queen!

Plate 193. *Politicians in a Country Bar* by James G. Clonney, oil, 1844. Courtesy New York Historical Association.

Clonney's New York State bar of 1844 shows close relationships with the earlier bars recorded by Krimmel, Kollner and Mount with their bare walls and floors. Here the shelves behind the bar hold an array of decanters plus boxes and a clock. Instead of the customary cuspidor, there is a spitting box filled with sand that serves as a resting place for two cigar butts. The furniture is interesting in that it is a mixture of old pieces of good quality and newer but simpler items. The Queen Anne chair by the door was probably a century old. The table has good legs of a more contemporary style, but the top seems to be rebuilt for plainness and strength. The ladderback or slatback chair with its rush seat might be entirely contemporary.

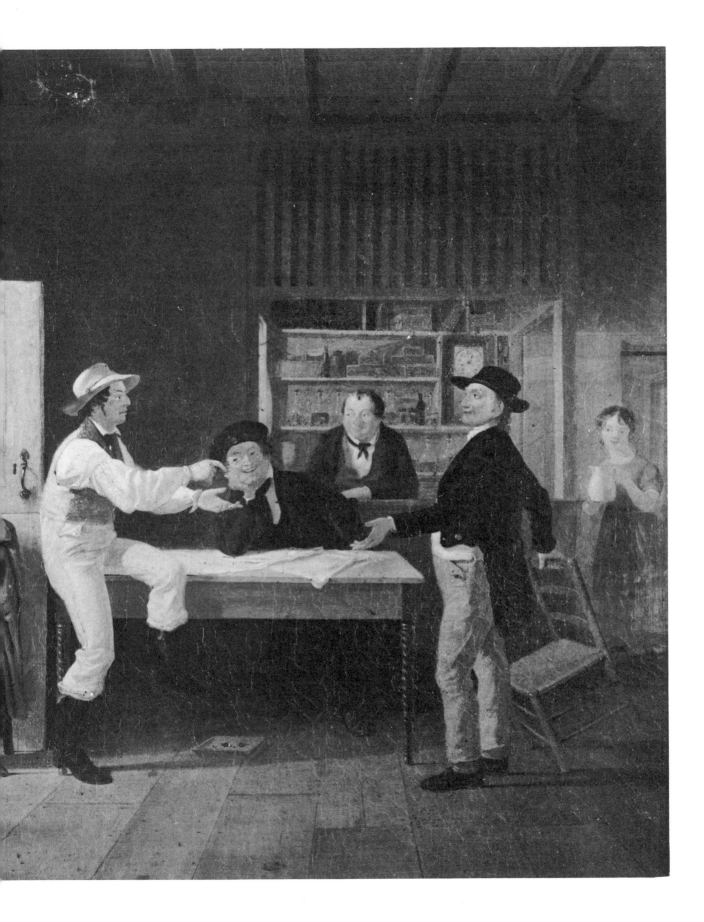

Plate 194. *The Card Players* by Richard Caton Woodville, oil, 1845. Courtesy of the Detroit Institute of Arts.

Travelers, playing cards, public notices and tobacco all seem to be characteristics of the country tavern. At least they appear in almost every surviving picture. In a rural community the tavern was, after all, the principal place to find transportation, obtain news, and enjoy social contact. Here the announcement sheets on the wall are exceptionally impressive, and the thoughtful proprietor has even provided a pitcher, slop bowl, towel, razor strop and looking glass for his patrons' convenience. The stove here sits on a metal plate that also holds a supply of firewood in addition to tongs and a broken pipe. On the stove top a tin kettle heats water for mixing hot toddies to warm the chilled wayfarers.

Plate 195. *Waiting for the Stage* by Richard Caton Woodville, oil, 1851. In the Collection of the Corcoran Gallery of Art.

Woodville was nearing the end of his painting career when he painted this scene of three assorted travelers waiting in a bar for the arrival of the stagecoach. It is a distinctly different tavern from the one he portrayed in the previous plate, but similar in the way that most smaller rural taverns must have resembled each other. In this case, however, the metal cuspidor looks like the very same specimen with its loose-fitting top. The stove is larger and placed in the typical box of sand rather than on a metal plate, and there is a fine birdcage on the wall. Here a slate hung on the bar supplements the notices stuck in the mirror frame as a means of public communication. The shelves behind the bar are dim, but close observation reveals labelled casks to supplement the bottles and decanters.

Plate 196. "Bar-room in California," woodcut from Frank Marryat, *Mountains and Molehills,* 1855. The Library of Congress.

San Francisco was a brand new boom town when Marryat visited it, but its barrooms could match anything in the more sophisticated eastern cities if this picture is to be believed. The chandeliers, the mirrored backbar with the rows of bottles on glass shelves, and the carved bar itself represent the highest development of the opulent bar style of the period. It is the customers who set this barroom apart. Older residents of Spanish descent mingle with American migrants from the East and even some of the newly arrived Chinese. Dogs, too, seem to have been welcome here as they were in most bars at the time, whether at a country tavern or an elaborate city spa.

Plate 197. *Temperance, But No Maine-Law* by A. Fay, lithograph, 1854. Courtesy, Museum of Fine Arts, Boston.

This exceptionally elaborate barroom graced The Gem Saloon at Worth Street and Broadway, New York City. The caption refers to a form of prohibition enacted in Maine. Even here, the dog, apparently a setter, is welcome amid the finery: the marble floor, marble-topped bar with its sculptured front and gas lamps. The huge mirror is framed apparently in gilt gesso which also provides the decoration for the dining booths at left. In keeping with a trend that favored art and curiosities for city bars, there is a case of stuffed birds so the patrons could absorb natural history with their tipples.

TEMPERANCE, BUT NO MAINE-LAW.

Plate 198. "The Refectories of New York.—The Newly Opened Bar-room of Messrs. Thomas Bros., Corner of Broadway and Washington Place," woodcut from *New York Illustrated News*, October 6, 1860. The New York Public Library.

Less opulent than the Gem Saloon, but still handsome was the barroom of the Thomas Brothers. Here the floor was marble or tile in a black and white checkerboard pattern, and the bar was quite probably carved walnut or mahogany. An interesting innovation is the method of hanging stemmed glasses upside down in the racks between the mirrors.

Plate 199. *How the Battle Was Won* by Enoch Wood Perry, oil, 1862. Collection of the Newark Museum.

In the barroom of this rural Louisiana tavern, probably just outside New Orleans, a wounded officer of the Confederate Army tells of his war experiences. The details of the room are dim, but they do indicate that Southern taverns differed little from their Northern counterparts at this period. Posters and pictures adorn the walls, and there is a clock behind the bar. The biggest difference, perhaps, is that the walls are papered rather than being left bare wood or plaster —and there is a grape arbor over the porch outside the door.

Plate 200. *Interior of George Hayward's Porter House, 187 Sixth Avenue, 1863* by E. D. Hawthorne, oil. Courtesy New-York Historical Society, New York City.

Officers and enlisted men of New York City regiments patronized Hayward's hostelry. By 1863 both the Highlanders and most of the zouaves had abandoned their distinctive uniforms in the field, but apparently they were still useful for social occasions. Hayward's barroom differed from most of its contemporaries in having a striped floor cloth, probably of painted canvas, instead of the usual marble or bare wood floor. Marble is present, however, in the panels on the wall and the front of the bar. And the walls are thickly hung with paintings. The device behind the bartender is not a cash register as it first appears but a drink dispenser, probably for coffee or other non-alcoholic beverages.

Plate 201. "Public Room at the 5th Ward Museum Hotel," lithograph by Major & Knapp for D. T. Valentine's *Manual*, 1864. The Library of Congress.

As its name suggests, the Museum Hotel carried the idea of exhibiting art, curiosities, natural history specimens and historical objects to its greatest heights. The bar is unusual in that it has a heavy rail to lean on just above counter height. Perhaps this is the precursor of the later brass foot rail that became so closely linked with a bar in popular memory about the turn of the century. The ceiling also is unusual in that it appears to have some sort of festoons of net or cloth that are inexplicable at this date. Otherwise it is a typical barroom of its era with a marble floor and the same low-back Windsor chairs of the captain's or Douglas patterns that also appear in the New Orleans and Porter House pictures in the previous plates.

Plate 202. *Warming Up* by Charles F. Blauvelt, oil, 1860–1870. Courtesy The Walters Gallery of Art.

Charles Blauvelt seemed to specialize in the simpler taverns and poorer people in contrast to the elegant New York City bars. Here a drover or coachman fights the cold in an exceptionally modest hostelry. One note of especial interest is the tin wall sconce with candle. It is a well-known type, but only Blauvelt has recorded its use in a tavern.

Plate 203. *Man Pouring Drink at a Bar* by Charles F. Blauvelt, oil, 1860–1870. Courtesy The Walters Gallery of Art.

This could quite probably represent the same bar as the one shown in the previous plate. The paneled front and framing seem to be the same. The cuspidor has been shifted and a different bench or stool shown, but these seem to be the principal differences. The back bar here is almost nonexistent. A few bottles and boxes rest on shelves in front of a window with half curtains on a string, and there are two more bottles on a side shelf. Again there is a tin candle sconce and a sign illegibly recommending an available tipple.

Plate 204.   *Waiting for the Train* by Charles F. Blauvelt, oil, 1860–1870. Courtesy the Maxwell Galleries, Ltd., San Francisco.

Here Blauvelt offers somewhat more detail of a crude and simple tavern. Every detail is calculated to emphasize the wretchedness of the establishment in contrast to the patient mother and her children. There is even a huge stack of firewood piled next to the bar while litter and dirt accentuate the shabbiness. Undoubtedly there were taverns this repulsive, but it seems highly unlikely that a scheduled railroad stop would fall into this category.

Plate 205. *"Eureka" Billiard Hall, Canyon City, Colorado,* photograph, c. 1875. Denver Public Library Western Collection; photo by Duhem Brothers.

The last picture in this appendix on inns and taverns offers an interesting contrast to the Latrobe watercolor of a Maryland billiard room some eighty years earlier (plate 188). Here the billiard table has moved into the barroom. The floor is still bare except for an oilcloth or rubber mat in front of the bar, but almost everything else has changed. The window has a shade, and the walls boast handsome architectural decorations. In keeping with the current fondness for growing plants in homes, this room also boasts a quantity of them—three on the window sill and three actually on the bar itself. It hardly seems likely that the bar top was the usual place for these plants since they would cut down on serving space. They may have been moved up there for the photograph—or even just to get them out of the way while the floor was being cleaned with no thought that this makeshift arrangement would be recorded for the puzzlement of posterity and permit this survey to close on a note of mystery.

INDEX OF ARTISTS

References are to plate numbers